WORKING IN SOCIAL CARE

Working in Social Care

A Systemic Approach

Dave Evans
Jeremy Kearney

arena

Published by
Arena
Ashgate Publishing Limited
Gower House
Croft Road
Aldershot
Hants GU11 3HR
England

Ashgate Publishing Company
Old Post Road
Brookfield
Vermont 05036
USA

British Library Cataloguing in Publication Data

Evans, Dave
    Working in social care: a systemic approach
    1. Social service
    I. Title   II. Kearney, Jeremy
    361.3

Library of Congress Catalog Card Number: 96-85391

ISBN 1 85742 355 0 (paperback)
ISBN 1 85742 354 2 (hardback)

Typeset by Raven Typesetters, Chester, Cheshire
and printed in Great Britain by Hartnolls Ltd, Bodmin.

Contents

List of figures

Acknowledgements

We would like to acknowledge the help, support and influence of a number of people in writing this book. First and foremost, we thank our families, Jackie, Lesley and Sarah, for their tolerance and active support. Our impetus to write this book owes much to the colleagues in New Zealand and England who participated in two parallel workshops in the late 1980s. Many other colleagues, including students, have stimulated the development of our thinking. We would particularly like to thank Jo Campling for her patience and guidance in this endeavour.

1 Introduction

Over recent years, a wide range of central government policy initiatives directed at the National Health Service, the personal social services and the criminal justice system have had a fundamental impact on the nature of service provision. Moreover, it is difficult to predict how these services will develop. We take the view that whatever the changes ahead, there will continue to be a wide range of workers in many different settings who will be committed to alleviating the social need experienced by others. Our own commitment to this aim as practitioners, trainers, supervisors and consultants working within a range of voluntary and statutory settings has led us to espouse a systemic approach as a framework for effective practice.

We have taken three steps to make this approach amenable and useful to the reader. First and foremost, we have attempted to orientate the ideas directly towards practice: by addressing the concrete issues of practice; by asking questions about the reader's practice, and by giving examples of our own and other people's practice. Second, we have tried to indicate ways in which a systemic approach, which focuses on interrelationships, contrasts with a currently dominant approach which focuses on separate people or units. Third, we have indicated some major disadvantages which may have been troubling the reader about two other major systems approaches – family therapy and the unitary model.

Key concepts

The title we have chosen includes four terms which take the reader to the heart of this book: 'systemic', 'approach', 'working' and 'social care'.

'Systemic'

Systems approaches to helping people in social need were particularly popular in the 1970s, following the development and dissemination of general systems theory (Von Bertalanffy, 1968). Several writers (Pincus and Minahan, 1973; Goldstein, 1973; Specht and Vickery, 1977) employed systems ideas in unitary or integrated models which had the subtext of integrating and unifying the differing methods and settings of the growing profession of social work. Some indicated the value of systems theory as a basis for therapy with families rather than individuals (Walrond-Skinner, 1976) or for work with the other relationships supporting people in need (Davies, 1977). Rubin (1973) simply celebrated these new ideas without fully exploring their implications for practice.

However, the context which saw the growth of these ideas also constrained their development. For example, the notion of integrated models for practice which can be adopted for all service user groups in generic social work teams has given way to the rediscovery of specialisms with particular legislative frameworks and knowledge requirements.

A central constraint of that period was the tendency to minimise the conflict and power differentials inherent in social systems, with some notable exceptions (Bailey and Brake, 1975). The systemic approach we propose in this book therefore seeks to recognise the context of oppression and discrimination which gives rise to and perpetuates much of the need experienced by the consumers of social care agencies.

The main concepts of this systemic approach are outlined in detail in Chapter 2. Of these, one central idea is that of *mutual interaction*: person A does not simply act towards a passive person B; person B will also attempt to influence person A. In a residential home for older people, for example, a care assistant may seek to persuade an older resident on to their feet in order to get ready for their bath. The older person may have other ideas, however: to watch a favourite TV programme or to await the visit of a relative. The resolution of these conflicting interests will depend upon a number of variables, including: the value base and practice skills of the worker; the frailty of the older person, and the degree of service user involvement in the management of the home. It will certainly be the case that the two participants in this two-way interaction will not have equal power.

'Resistant' is one adjective often used by workers to describe such a resident. It clearly reveals the workers' fundamental misapprehension that service users should simply comply with workers' wishes and not exercise whatever power they have at their disposal to pursue their own wishes.

'Manipulative' is another similarly blinkered description of service users' actions. In this case, workers often find themselves at the receiving end of some effective use of power by the service user – for example, having sought the support of the officer in charge. Workers are thus hindered in using their power to pursue their own wishes, or perhaps even prevented from doing so.

'Resistant' and 'manipulative' are therefore both epithets which give warning that a worker has not been sufficiently aware of (a) the two-way nature of interactions and (b) the power differentials inherent in those interactions. Seen from the perspective of the 'resistant' or 'manipulative' service user, the interaction will assume a very different complexion. Indeed, at times, the service user may well apply the mirror adjective to the worker:

> service user 'resistant' = worker 'manipulative'
> service user 'manipulative' = worker 'resistant'

Another idea central to a systemic approach is that of *context* by which we mean the relevant aspects of the environment. Context can be 'synchronic' – that is, at one point in time. At the same time as writing this book, we have other roles as, for example, workers and husbands, which influence and are influenced by the writing. Context can also be 'diachronic' – that is, extended through time. Our writing on a given day will be influenced by a previous late night or the prospect of a future holiday. These two contextual axes intersect (see Figure 1.1).

The specific context which brought us together as co-writers included a growing shared awareness of the constraining and limited use to which potentially more useful systems ideas had been put. As social work students and teachers, we had been struck by the limitations of unitary models of practice, based on systems theory. As experienced family therapy practitioners and trainers, we became aware of the inappropriate constraints imposed by developing systems ideas in clinical settings. (These criticisms are discussed in Chapter 2.) A further context within which we have joined to work

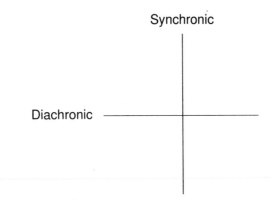

Figure 1.1   Two contextual axes

on this book is a growing awareness of the profound influence power plays in all human interactions. Systems theory and family therapy have both been slow to develop an analysis of power.

It is this focus on power which leads us, like other writers (Howe, 1987; Cordern and Preston-Shoot, 1987a; Lishman, 1994) to draw on the existing body of social work consumer research. In seeking to address the power imbalance in favour of professional workers and their agencies and against service users, it would seem essential to listen carefully to what those service users have to say about workers and agencies (Wallace and Rees, 1984). This is not to suggest that all policies and practices should be framed exclusively by service users, but that they should have some influence. Although it was written over a decade ago, Rees and Wallace's *Verdicts on Social Work* (1982) provides some seminal evidence, not only in its comprehensiveness but also in its orientation to issues of power, and is cited on several occasions throughout this book, along with other summaries of consumer studies, including Fisher (1983) and Cheetham et al. (1992).

'Approach'

This book does not contain a new theory: it is not a highly abstract set of ideas which seeks to explain existing phenomena or to predict future events. It simply describes an approach, comprising an interrelated set of ideas which are orientated to help workers develop their practice. It is true that the approach draws from a theoretical base, as will be demonstrated in Chapter 2. However, we have been concerned more with the usefulness of ideas than their abstract coherence or status.

The value of theory in social care has been much debated. Research has consistently indicated how little overt use experienced workers in the personal social services make of theory (DHSS, 1978; Carew, 1979). Some of this underuse can perhaps be explained, as Davies (1984) suggests, by educators, writers and other brokers of theory not making sufficiently meaningful links between theory and practice. It has even been argued that people in academic settings have a vested interest in demonstrating the usefulness of theory (Pilalis, 1986; Evans, 1987b).

As might be expected from our current posts in academic institutions, our own views on theory are more sympathetic than many workers in the personal social services. Like Coulshed (1988), we see the relationship between theory and practice as an interaction, wherein the one influences the other. Although the relationship is frequently conceived of as one-way, whereby theory influences practice, it is also the case that the experiences of practice give rise to the development and refinement of theory. Our approach has arisen precisely from maintaining this mutual interaction between abstract ideas and concrete practices.

We are also in agreement with Paley (1987), who asserts that the question which most concerns workers is not 'How does theory relate to practice?' but 'What ideas can help me in my practice?' For this reason, we offer a set of helpful ideas which constitute an approach.

'Working'

Everyone seeks to alleviate social need. Sometimes they experience it first-hand themselves or it is experienced by someone else with whom they have an ongoing relationship, such as a neighbour, friend or relative. These efforts form only a part of much wider processes in life. Indeed, if people only concentrated on alleviating social need to the exclusion of all other facets of life, they would risk living considerably unbalanced lives. This everyday relationship to social need could be called 'living with'.

However, certain people also seek to address the social need experienced by other people with whom they have no other ongoing relationship. They do so as part of their work, as a volunteer, a freelance worker or a paid employee. In this book, we refer to this particular relationship as 'working with', and consider it to be of a different nature to the more everyday relationship of 'living with' social need.

Of course, there are many similarities between the two sets of relationships, particularly when the work takes place in informal group care settings. Indeed, there is evidence from the clients of social workers that they prefer workers who minimise the differences: who are more like friends and less like professionals (Mayer and Timms, 1970). It is our experience, as teachers, that social work students early in their careers can often fulfil this preference but are unlikely to be able to sustain it throughout their career. One of the aims of this book is to help workers maximise their potential advantages as workers and minimise the inherent disadvantages.

Social care

In using the term 'social care', we are seeking to emphasise the communalities between two sets of workers within the statutory, voluntary and private sectors of the personal social services. Social care workers and social workers are often differentiated in terms of tasks. Hugman (1991) makes the useful distinction between workers who 'care for' people, often involving direct physical care, and those who 'care about' people, involving less direct physical care. Social care workers and social workers also differ according to their work settings, training, status and, particularly, salary levels. Bamford (1990) further distinguishes between the two, albeit rather unconvincingly, in terms of, respectively, maintenance and change. With the increased emphasis on social care planning in social work (NISW, 1982; Griffiths, 1988; NHS and

Community Care Act, 1990), however, and the development of a cohesive training strategy by the National Council for Vocational Qualifications, these differences are being eroded.

It is our view that the similarities between these two sets of workers outweigh the differences. Not only do they often possess similar values and attributes, they also operate within similar social situations. These situations can be described in two main ways: 'social need' or 'social problems'.

Payne (1991) argues persuasively that 'need' is a key concept in social work. A similar claim can be made in all the work performed by social care workers. As Payne suggests, the concept is a highly complex one, and its complexity stems from the differing answers to two central questions:

- What are needs?
- Who defines needs?

Maslow (1970) distinguishes between two distinct sets of need: those which ensure survival (basic physical and psychological needs) and those which promote the person's self-actualisation (intellectual and creative needs). Payne (1991, p. 29) makes an alternative dichotomy between needs which are 'internal drives' (for example, for food) and those which are 'socially defined' (for example, good health care).

What is common to both categorisations is the moral imperative implicit in the term 'need'. Once something is defined as a 'need', it becomes morally incumbent on people to seek to fulfil it. 'Need' is thus not the language of objective description but the language of moral obligation. Like other moral language ('must', 'should', 'ought to'), it is used to influence other people's behaviour, presumably to fulfil that need.

The second question, 'Who defines needs?', focuses on who is trying to influence whom. Bradshaw's (1972) taxonomy of social need gives some indications of who defines needs:

- normative need – defined by an 'expert' or professional;
- felt need – defined by the individual person experiencing it;
- expressed need – defined by the individual, and often another person, in applying for services;
- comparative need – defined, for example, by policymakers or managers in seeking equitable service delivery.

Increasingly, legislators are also attempting to define need ('children in need' in the Children Act, 1989 and 'assessment of need' in the NHS and Community Care Act, 1990).

This second question takes us to the heart of the issue of power: who has the power to determine that a certain condition *must* be attended to. Will vulnerable individuals be in a position to determine their circumstances as 'need' in order to elicit a response, or will powerful workers, managers and politicians determine 'need' for quite different reasons, such as the allocation of inadequate resources or the increased privatisation of social welfare? The history of the implementation of the NHS and Community Care Act (1990) suggests that the tension in defining need still remains, but that service users will not be allowed to determine need alone.

The inadequacy of resources in social welfare points to one of the deficiencies in the term 'need'. On the one hand, 'need' implies a moral imperative; on the other, inadequate resources determine that this imperative will not be fulfilled in all cases. It is clearly misleading for central government, agencies and their workers to raise an expectation that situations *must* be alleviated when they clearly *cannot* be.

A second deficiency in the term 'need' is inherent in Bradshaw's (1972) distinction between 'felt' and 'expressed' need. Much 'need' remains in the private domain and is not brought to the attention of personal social service agencies, whether statutory, voluntary or private. Indeed, many people suffering severe physical needs (for shelter or protection) may be unaware of other 'higher' needs, in Maslow's (1970) terms. Clearly, the level of need which is 'felt' and not 'expressed', or which is even 'beyond awareness', would be beyond the scope of the personal social services to assess. Personal social service agencies are already stretched by dealing with need as it is overtly expressed to them, without seeking to discover covert need.

An alternative view of these social situations construes them as 'problems'. Perlman (1957) introduced a problem-solving approach into the long-term social work methods of that time. It has found successors in task-centred, behavioural and cognitive-behavioural approaches (Howe, 1987; Coulshed, 1991) and is still congruent with the current emphasis on cost-effectiveness. However, the term 'problem' has the one principal disadvantage that it concentrates on difficulties and deficits rather than strengths and opportunities (see Chapter 3). This difficulty is particularly pronounced when people themselves are labelled as 'problems', rather than simply being seen to be experiencing problems. The expressions 'problem families' and 'problem child' of earlier decades fell into this trap. For this reason, we favour the term 'need' over 'problem'.

'Need' is 'social', in our view, when it occurs within the relationship between people and their social environment – the institutions, the individuals and the physical settings which surround them. The needs of disabled children will arise partly from the children themselves – the range of physical abilities available to them and their emotional and intellectual responses to that range – partly from a range of deficits in the child's physical and social environment and, particularly, from any mismatch between the two. 'Social' is not simply external to the individual, as Durkheim (1938) suggests, but comprises the interplay between individual and social environment.

'Social need' can be contrasted with other forms of need: physical, psychological, medical, educational. However, there will clearly be some overlap between them. A sick person may have a *prima facie* need for medical care. Their illness may also prevent them looking after themselves physically and domestically, thus giving rise to a range of social needs. As the medical needs are met, so the social needs will diminish. Likewise, proper social care may hasten a recovery in health.

Why a systemic approach is particularly relevant today

Within the personal social services, workers have to be aware of highly complex contexts. The crisis in welfare arising from a growing gulf between needs and resources has stimulated the growth of a 'mixed economy of welfare', contributed to by informal carers and the voluntary and commercial sectors, as well as the state (Munday, 1989). The increasingly complex patterns of interaction between these sectors make it impossible for workers in social care agencies to act in isolation.

Moreover, the conflicting values within these sectors, coupled with a disturbing convergence of right- and left-wing ideologies in accepting this pluralism, has placed a high premium on workers determining their own value position. Howe (1987) described an interesting 'classificatory' phase in the development of social work theories, to which he and Whittington and Holland (1985) make key contributions. It is likely that the recognition of a need to classify the value base of social work theories is a direct response to a period of growing pluralism. Essential to a systemic approach, we believe, is a recognition of the worker's own value position in relation to conflicting contextual pressures.

Another trend which also suggests the increasing relevance of a systemic approach has been the growth of partnerships. This has been a major endeavour of the Conservative administrations of the past decade and a half in the UK: between academic institutions and service agencies; between purchasers, providers and consumers; between the formal and informal carers of both children and adults in need; between health and social care services. It is tempting to see this pressure towards partnership as a deliberate erosion of the power of established interest groups to enhance the greater power of central government. Whatever the cause, workers in social services agencies will need models that enable them to understand and work effectively within the patterns of these complex partnerships.

How this book is organised

Chapter 2 makes a central statement about the position of this book. It charts the development of systems ideas in social work and other disciplines, and it examines in some detail two other major systems approaches which have had some influence on workers, particularly social workers – the unitary model and family therapy. It explores the contexts which gave rise to those approaches and indicates the deficiencies which stem from those contexts. It then seeks to clarify our own systemic approach, placing it in a context which acknowledges power structures.

Chapter 3 specifies several principles which we have found useful guides for our own practice and in training or teaching others.

Chapter 4 focuses on one specific interaction which is at the heart of all social care work – between the service user, the worker and the worker's agency. The nature of that triangular relationship is explored at a given point in time.

Chapter 5 continues an examination of the relationship between those three participants, but as they interact over time, in the different phases of working in social care. The focus is also widened to include the multi-agency context of work. The last phase is 'ending', and it provides a fitting context for also drawing the book to a close.

In writing this book, we have accepted its limitations as an interactional channel of communication with its readers. In Chapters 3, 4 and 5 we invite the reader to answer a number of questions about their particular work context, which are intended to bring the ideas closer to their practice.

2 The development of a systemic approach

This is primarily a book about practice, offering some practical ways to work with different social needs in a range of social work contexts. However, in order to practise effectively and ethically, it is important to be clear about the theories and values that underpin that practice.

In Chapter 1, we indicated the importance of an awareness of context as a key principle of a systemic approach, and therefore it is useful to put systemic ideas in context by outlining their historical and theoretical background. In order to provide this framework for systemic ideas and their relationship to social work practice, this chapter examines a number of different contexts:

1   the historical development of social work;
2   the emergence of a new theoretical framework from the 1940s onwards;
3   the way systems theory has been used in social work practice, particularly in relation to the 'unitary' approach and family therapy.

The historical development of social work

We do not intend to present a detailed history of social work, as this topic has already been covered elsewhere (Seed, 1973; Yelloly, 1980; Jones, 1983; Howe, 1987; Barber, 1990) but rather to identify some of the important strands that have been significant in creating the context of present-day practice in the personal social services.

Arising from the long traditions of philanthropy and charity, there were a number of attempts to organise social welfare in the nineteenth century. These included: the development of social administration by the state, as illustrated by such actions as the introduction of the Poor Law and improvements in public health, hygiene and housing; the charity organisation move-

11

ment, which began to organise philanthropy in a scientific and efficient manner and devised principles to guide the provision of help for people in need, and the work of social reformers such as Robert Owen, Elizabeth Fry and Mary Carpenter, who attempted to produce social change by direct social action, such as visiting people in prisons and workhouses, and setting up schools or whole communities.

In his overview of the development of theoretical ideas in social work, Barber (1990) makes a useful distinction between what he calls the 'pre-generalist' and 'generalist' eras, and describes a 'discontinuous shift in theorising' which took place in the 1970s with a move to unitary and systemic approaches.

The pre-generalist era, which Barber traces back to the work of Mary Richmond and her book *Social Diagnosis* (Richmond, 1917), was the beginning of the psychosocial approach (Barber, 1990, p. 15). This approach emphasised a very individualistic form of social work based on investigation, diagnosis and treatment. The concentration on the individual continued with the influence of psychoanalysis and the ideas of Freud, which became very significant in social work, first in the USA in the 1920s and then in the UK from the 1940s onwards (Yelloly, 1980).

What has been called the 'functionalist' school of Taft and Robinson emphasised the 'here and now' of the current situation and the 'function' of the responding worker or agency (Howe, 1987). It placed more weight on working with the client and on the importance of the relationship itself as being therapeutic. Other approaches, such as the problem-solving approach of Perlman (1957), which concentrated on dealing with the specific problem at hand, attempted to bring together some of the aspects of earlier models and also had links with such time-limited models as task-centred casework and crisis intervention (Coulshed, 1991).

As Barber (1990) indicates, all these pre-generalist models have certain characteristics in common which limit their ability to achieve change: a concentration on the individual; an emphasis on pathology and a deficit model of human behaviour; an acceptance of the prevailing social structures, and a very limited view of the influence of the client's wider contexts. By the 1950s, therefore, social work could be seen to emphasise the individual, intrapsychic processes, and the development of a professional function for social work.

What Barber (1990) calls 'generalist' approaches – more often described as 'unitary' or 'integrated' approaches – became very influential in social work in the 1970s. The work of Goldstein (1973), Pincus and Minahan (1973), Davies (1977) and Specht and Vickery (1977), among others, looked at the application of systems theory to social work practice. The reasons why this interest developed included: a feeling that many of the psychodynamically-based models had proved inadequate; a growth of interest in how more sociologically-based theories could be used in social work (Payne, 1991), and a belief that there were too many unclarified and diverse theories in social work. Therefore, there was a need to establish basic principles and a unified approach that would apply to all methods of social work practice (Howe, 1987).

A similar shift was reflected at a political level by the recommendations of the Seebohm Report (1968), moving from a model where in separate departments (children, health, welfare) dealt with different service user groups towards the introduction of local authority social services departments providing a generic service to the whole community (NISW, 1982).

Within the 'interactionist' school of sociology (Becker, 1963), particularly within their work on deviance, there was a clear focus beyond the individual. For the interactionist school, the delinquent behaviour of young people was not inherent in the individual but was a result of how society viewed them. In other words, it was necessary to look at the relationship (the interaction) between those who are seen as deviant and those who describe them as deviant (Howe, 1987). These ideas came into social work teaching in the 1970s as part of the shift from a psychodynamic to a sociological perspective.

Other ways of thinking were also focusing more on wider social contexts and less on individuals. The development of radical social work in the late 1960s and early 1970s focused in particular on class and poverty (Bailey and Brake, 1975). However, as has been pointed out by later writers, there were significant gaps in the initial, radical social work analysis in relation to race, gender and other oppressions (Dominelli and McLeod, 1989; Langan and Lee, 1989).

This historical background indicates a context within the broad field of social work which offered the possibility of using systemic ideas. In particular, what Barber (1990) calls the 'discontinuous shift' from pre-generalist to generalist ideas can be seen as significant in creating more emphasis on the 'social context'.

The emergence of a new theoretical framework

The theoretical foundations in a systemic approach can be seen as arising from a number of different influences which emerged after the Second World War. Although these ideas developed in a number of unrelated fields – such as computer science, mathematics, systems analysis and communications theory – they were linked by a shift in thinking, or a 'new paradigm', to use Kuhn's (1970) phrase. A paradigm can be seen as 'a fundamental world view' (Johnson, 1981) or the 'system of ideas, beliefs and attitudes which provide both the background and framework for theory development and associated research endeavours' (Chamberlain, 1977, p. 1). In terms of therapeutic work, this shift in 'world view' was to an approach which was concerned with an emphasis on interdependence and interaction rather than individual and isolated responses, and on information rather than energy.

These seemingly unrelated developments contributed to an intellectual climate in which the psychosocial context in which human beings live became a focus of attention for researchers and clinicians in the social sciences (Haley, 1971). One writer has characterised this shift in thinking in relation to therapy as a 'concern with the interdependence of seemingly opposing entities – unit and context, sickness and health, part and whole, deviant and normal, individual and community' (Walrond-Skinner, 1976).

The network of theories which has led to the development of a systemic approach includes systems theory, cybernetics and communications theory, and the main practice models have been the unitary approach and family therapy. We will describe the basic principles of each of these theories and models before looking at what influence they have had on work in social care and the development of a systemic approach.

Systems theory

A systemic approach uses some of the ideas and concepts of systems theory as a means of thinking about and understanding particular systems people are involved in or are dealing with, whether these happen to be families, groups, residential establishments, agencies or wider social systems. For our purposes in this book, it is not necessary to describe in detail the complexities of systems theory, as these are the subject of a large number of texts (Walrond-Skinner, 1976; Barker, 1981; Burnham, 1986; Preston-Shoot and Agass, 1990), but we will outline some of the main ideas that are of significance.

The overall theoretical framework was given the name 'general systems theory' by Ludwig von Bertalanffy (1968), and it was hoped that it would provide a general science of pattern and organisation which could unify differing ideas within general theoretical concepts. It is a very broad-based theory which attempts to 'provide a working model for conceptualising phenomena which do not lend themselves to explanation by the mechanistic reductionism of classical science' (Walrond-Skinner, 1976). Therefore, in general terms, the definition of what constitutes a system is very broad, and the word 'system' has been defined as 'a set of objects together with the relationships between the objects and between their attributes' (Hall and Fagen, 1956).

In relation to human life, the key concepts of systems theory provide a shift from the focus on the person in isolation to the person in context. Systems theory sees the individual as existing in a web of relationships which they both influence and are influenced by, and any behaviour needs to be understood in the context of these relationships.

Clearly, people are interacting in many different systems – such as the family, school, work and others – all the time, and in order to differentiate between these systems, the concept of a 'boundary' is used. This is a means of delineating different systems as well as looking at the relationships between them. Some boundaries are generally clear and remain fairly stable over time – for example, the boundary around the family as a key social system or the border between two different countries; others are harder to define and change continuously – for example, the people who travel on the London Underground on any particular day.

One of the most important implications of systems theory is that people both influence and are influenced by the systems with which they interact. This means that those of us involved with people as teachers, care workers or managers cannot remain objective and outside the systems we work with; we are always in some kind of relationship with them.

Human systems develop patterns of relating over time. From a systems point of view, the notion of linear causality is replaced by the concept of circular causality. In human terms, the notion of linear causality implies that incident A causes behaviour B as an effect: for example, 'Because they were treated badly as a child, they committed the crime'; whereas systems theory would say that there is reciprocal influence between all parts of the system, and all play some part in the outcome: 'Their behaviour as a child had an influence on how their parents treated them.' The explanation for the behaviour could be found in the interaction between the person, their family and the wider social systems. From this perspective, no individual can operate in total isolation and control the behaviour of a system; rather, they are part of a process which involves all members of that system.

This concept of circular causality has been used by some writers to argue for a highly relativistic stance in relation to human actions and to suggest that everyone in any system has equal influence over what happens (Dell, 1982, Boscolo et al., 1987). Of course, this approach ignores power imbalances inherent in issues of gender, ethnic origins, disability and other oppressions where there is a structural inequality which affects the relationships between the parts of the system. The most obvious example is in cases of abuse and violence against women and children, where it is ethically unacceptable to say that the woman or child plays an equal part in the system by 'asking to be abused'.

We would argue that such a 'neutral' position is not an essential characteristic of a systemic approach. Any systemic analysis has to pay attention to the 'parts' and 'relationships' that make up a particular system: power is an essential component of relationships between human beings.

Cybernetics

Cybernetics is the science of machines and how they operate, in particular the processes of regulation and control based on the exchange of information (Ashby, 1952; Buckley, 1968). A very important idea which comes from the theory of cybernetics is the concept of self-regulation, or *feedback*. This means that 'part of a system's output is reintroduced into the system as information about the output' (Watzlawick et al., 1967). A good example of a cybernetic machine is a guided missile, which uses the information it receives from outside – wind speed, landscape, temperature – and compares this with the instructions that have been programmed into it in order to make adjustments to its speed and direction. In other words, the *output* (the flight plan programmed into the missile) is compared with the *input* (the information coming in from the world outside) and so changes the output (the missile changes speed, alters direction).

In human systems, all of us use the responses we receive from others as indicators to adjust our behaviours and actions. This is a continual process which takes place on multiple levels simultaneously, both consciously and unconsciously, and can be viewed as feedback. A simple example of this process occurs when a male service user is generally regarded by staff as 'aggressive' and is thus approached anxiously by staff when they have to deal with him. This in turn makes the service user suspicious and uncertain, and he responds negatively to what is experienced as an unhelpful approach. As a result, the workers' original perception of a 'resistant client' is confirmed. This process can either increase or decrease the initial response. In the example above, the workers' responses help to increase the level of activity: this is known as 'positive' feedback. This does not mean that it is 'good', but rather that the initial response serves to create an increasing spiral of interaction, which in this example can lead to violence.

Communication theory

For any approach based on interaction, the question of how any system interacts – the communication between the different parts – is vital. With the development of general systems theory, there was a shift in thinking from models based on transmission of energy to ones based on information.

Freud's theory is based on an energy model, where the individual's behaviour is caused by fundamental drives within the personality (Freud, 1973). When these drives are repressed, they emerge as symptomatic behaviour. However, in a feedback model of information exchange, where the interaction is not based on energy but on information, there is a circular process, where A's behaviour affects B, then B's response in turn influences A, and so on in a continual process.

The work of Gregory Bateson has been very important in developing a communication model of interaction, and he gives a clear example of the difference between a model based on energy and one based on information:

> If I kick a stone, the movement of the stone is energised by the act, but if I kick a dog, the behaviour of the dog may indeed be partly conservative – he may travel along a Newtonian trajectory if kicked hard enough, but this is mere physics. What is important is that he may exhibit responses which are energised not by the kick but by his metabolism; he may turn and bite. (Bateson, 1973, p. 200)

In other words, the dog will not only respond to the physical energy of the kick but also the information contained in the action.

Another aspect of communication theory is the ability of human beings to communicate different messages simultaneously, by using a tone of voice or a body posture which contradicts the verbal message. Bateson and his colleagues (Ruesch and Bateson, 1968; Bateson, 1973) introduced the concept of meta-communication to describe messages that convey information at different levels. Irony is a well-known example of this: ' "I find you really interesting," she said with a yawn.'

As Watzlawick et al. (1967) suggest, every behaviour is a communication which provokes a feedback consisting of another behaviour-communication. This acknowledgement of the relationship between behaviour and communication has very important implications for understanding how human systems operate and, as a result, to understanding how to help them change. Much of this understanding comes from the work of the Bateson group in Palo Alto, and their development of the double-bind theory, especially in relation to schizophrenia (Bateson et al., 1956). However, as Weakland has pointed out, the value of the Bateson group's work was that:

> there was the beginning of a close identification of communication and behaviour as two sides of the same coin . . . a recognition that the most important aspect of social behaviour is its communicative effect and that communication is a major factor in the ordering of behaviour socially. (Weakland, 1974, p. 274)

This has important implications for working with people: problems between people, or between organisations and people, are often described as being the result of a lack of communication, whereas the real source of the problem may be that people do not like the information contained in the communication they are receiving – for example, the message implied by their partner's silence or the organisation's non-response. The importance of communication in working with people is well summed up by Bateson's concise phrase 'You cannot not communicate.'

These ideas have found their way by differing routes into the broad field of social care over the last four decades. However, the impact of these ideas has been very variable, and it would be hard to argue that they have fundamentally influenced the general direction of practice in any specific way. We identify two main areas where the influence of these ideas can be seen: (1) the unitary or integrated approach, and (2) family therapy.

The unitary approach

In the early 1970s, a number of writers (Goldstein, 1973; Pincus and Minahan, 1973; Vickery, 1974) drew on systems theory in an attempt to bring together the diverse range of theories that were then being used in social work. Their aim was to develop a unified approach that could then be applied to all methods of social work practice. For this reason, the approach was known as the 'unitary' or 'integrated' approach.

There were a number of reasons why this approach achieved prominence in social work, and particularly in social work education. One was that it offered a possible solution to the problem of making sense of the diverse range of theoretical ideas that were prevalent in social work up to that time (Howe, 1987). Second, research seemed to show that many of the psychodynamically-based theories were ineffective (Mayer and Timms, 1970; Mullen and Dumpson, 1972) and that clients were unclear about the aims and purposes of social work. A model based on more sociologically-orientated theories and attempting to provide a unifying theme to social work was conceptually very attractive. Third, the Seebohm Report (1968) had initiated the unification of the personal social services: separate, specialist services became one 'generic' service provided by the local authority. The early 1970s was thus a time when social work and related occupations grew in size and status in the UK. A unifying theoretical approach was attractive in order to underpin this much broader unification of service provision and hence to support the acquisition of greater occupational power.

Within this context, writers such as Pincus and Minahan (1973) and Goldstein (1973) in the USA and Vickery (1974), Specht and Vickery (1977) and Olsen (1978) in the UK attempted to provide such a unified theory. Their books presented theoretical models based on systems theory and were proposed as broad frameworks for integrating disparate approaches within social work. The aim was to develop an approach to practice that could be used in any work setting.

As Pincus and Minahan stated:

> regardless of the many forms social work practice can take, there is a common core of concepts, skills, tasks and activities which are essential to the practice of social work and represent a base from which the practitioner can build. (Pincus and Minahan, 1973, p. xi)

The focus of the unitary model was to try to look at service users in their social setting and to concentrate on the interaction between the individual and their environment. Although this approach became quite popular in the 1970s, particularly in educational settings, it is not clear how much influence these writers had on actual practice. However, in our view, one important adverse effect that these writers had was to create a strong association in social work between the unitary approach and systems theory. In many cases, they were regarded as one and the same thing. It is our view that this has been a considerable limitation on the development of the positive and creative use of systemic ideas in practice.

One of the problems of the close association of the unitary approach with systems theory is that the unitary approach is seriously limited because the systems theory it draws on is based in the social theory of functionalism and, in particular, the work of Talcott Parsons (1951). Leonard (1975) has pointed out that this is very much 'a conservative consensus-orientated' ideology of stability and order rather than a model of conflict and change. Parsons' theory of structural functionalism focuses on the maintenance of stability in a system and how the individual carries out their function within this overall system (Langan, 1985).

As Mancoske says in summarising the criticisms of systems theory in sociology:

> Critics claim that Parsons' action theory is less a systems theory than a statics theory. It is not empirically verifiable as developed, and is so abstract and vague that concepts are undefinable. The emphasis of action theory is on function, not process of intervention, and this negates the meaning of systems. (Mancoske, 1981, pp. 714–15)

This same criticism has also been levelled at the use of systems theory by the promoters of the unitary approach in social work. Ross and Bilson (1989) point out that Pincus and Minahan:

> leave out most of the essential components of systems thinking from their analysis of social work. In particular their work does not use concepts such as interconnectedness and feedback. In our view these issues are at the heart of ideas of change in social work and theoretical perspectives that do not address them carry a fatal flaw. (Ross and Bilson, 1989, p. 19)

We would agree with this view, and we feel that the influence of unitary approaches has not been useful in developing a systemic model of practice within social work.

A number of other writers have also criticised the use of a unitary approach in social work as being: overinclusive and too general (Triseliotis, 1987); supposedly relativistic and neutral, yet in reality maintaining the dominant patriarchical ideology in relation to women's roles (Langan, 1985); essentially reformist rather than empowering (Ahmed et al., 1986), and not providing any guidelines about what to do in order to influence systems and change them (Jordan, 1981). These weaknesses are in fact the result of the underlying theory on which the approach is based – functionalism. As Howe points out, this leads to a conservative and consensus-based model of practice: 'one in which the social worker functions to maintain society and its people in a relatively stable state' (Howe, 1987, p. 54).

However, some have argued for a more positive view of the unitary approach and its potential for producing change. Evans (1976) is enthusiastic about the possibilities of a unitary approach which constitutes a shift from a predominantly 'individualistic' model to an 'interactionist' one. Evans points out that the comprehensive critique of the functionalist approach of Talcott Parsons had been generalised to systems theory as a whole, and thus led to its relative neglect. Therefore, in his criticism of Pincus and Minahan's and Goldstein's use of systems theory, he supports Leonard's (1975) view that the consensus model of society is not inherent in 'the logic of systems theory' but rather in the way the proponents of the unitary approach interpret it. His conclusion is that the unitary approach, in the broad sense and not necessarily as it has been presented by particular authors, has 'provided a holistic conceptual model of social work practice which is not only useful in practice but confronts social workers with a range of issues concerning the theoretical and value base of their work' (Evans, 1976, p. 182).

Writing from a radical social work perspective, Leonard (1975) acknowledges that Pincus and Minahan and Goldstein do not question the dominant assumptions of the nature of society and that they accept a conservative, consensus-orientated ideology. Despite this, he feels that it is possible to 'rescue systems theory from the grasp of apologists of existing institutions and to use it for the purposes of understanding and changing these institutions' (Leonard, 1975, p. 48) and that radical social workers could 'build an integrated model of radical social work on the basis of a critical evaluation' of the work of these writers. He identifies that the unitary approach has achieved some success in shifting the 'focus of attention from individual or group pathology to that of interaction', while it has ignored the 'power distribution within and between systems' and their 'controlling and oppressive role'.

However, it should be noted that Langan (1985), writing from a feminist perspective, is dismissive of Leonard's efforts to operate the unitary approach in a radical way. She argues that any attempt to rescue systems theory is always flawed as, in her view, the basic principle of social systems theory is to assume that the parts interrelate in a manner that maintains equilibrium.

This tension between those writers who sensed some potential within the unitary approach to develop radical models of practice and those who still see it as inherently conservative is well illustrated in a recent publication by

Bandana Ahmad (1992). She describes a case example illustrating how what she calls the 'unitary approach' was used in an empowering way in work with a young black woman who was identified as having a 'problem' with the predominantly white staff of the day nursery her child was attending.

In her analysis of the case, Ahmad outlines a range of strategies adopted by the worker who was called in to deal with the 'problem'. These included linking the young woman in with a black women's group, as well as some direct counselling. It also involved writing a report suggesting ways of establishing a multicultural policy for all day nurseries and developing anti-racist practice guidelines and training procedures.

In the sense that the worker focused on the wider context of the 'problem', utilised a range of different techniques and skills and connected with resource systems in the local community, this is an example of some aspects of the unitary approach. However, what makes it fundamentally different to the value base of the unitary approach is that issues of power are addressed directly. Ahmad makes it quite clear that only by utilising the approach within a consistent black perspective is it of any value. She emphasises:

> I firmly believe that without a Black perspective, [the] Unitary Model of Social Work can neither claim to be an 'integrated model of social work', nor can it fulfil its empowering potentials – whether for Black clients or White clients. (Ahmad, 1992, p. 61)

So it is only by giving the unitary approach a committed value base that it becomes useful. However, by making the commitment to such a value base, the approach then takes a position which is contested and forces workers to choose between different theoretical models: that is to say, the approach is not unified or integrated.

Our own view of the unitary approach is that it created a limiting context in social work which excluded more dynamic systemic ideas such as interconnectedness, circularity, feedback and information exchange. Its potential was also limited by the underlying conservative value base of functionalism and an overriding political aim of unifying and professionalising social work. As a result, the potential of systems theory to be used as a building block towards empowering action in social care practice was highly restricted.

Family therapy

Systemic ideas have been developed much more thoroughly and rigorously by theorists within the field of family therapy, and a number of coherent models of practice have emerged which have proved to be effective and useful. These models include: structural family therapy (Minuchin, 1974), strategic therapy (Haley, 1976; Madanes, 1981), Milan systemic therapy (Palazzoli et al., 1980; Boscolo et al., 1987), solution-focused therapy (De Shazer, 1982, 1985), narrative therapy (White and Epston, 1990) and the reflecting team (Andersen, 1990). The ideas and practices have also been developed by many writers in the UK (Walrond-Skinner, 1976; Barker, 1981; Treacher and Carpenter, 1984; Carpenter and Treacher, 1989, 1993; Campbell and Draper, 1985; Burnham, 1986). However, we believe that the context of family therapy has limited the application of these ideas in social care work, and we will examine these limitations later in this chapter. First, we wish to examine briefly the key ideas behind the development of family therapy thinking and practice.

There is already a large and rapidly expanding body of literature on the history and development of family therapy (Walrond-Skinner, 1976; Broderick and Schrader, 1981; Barker, 1981; Hoffman, 1981). We intend to concentrate on a number of thinkers and ideas that are of particular importance in relation to the development of a systemic approach.

Undoubtedly, one of the most significant figures was Gregory Bateson. Although originally he was not involved with either families or therapy, his influence was very important, as he played a major role in linking new ideas to therapeutic practice. He began his career as an anthropologist, and during his field research he developed ideas about how the societies he was studying were organised. His research led him to become involved in a series of multi-disciplinary meetings in the late 1940s and early 1950s called 'the Macy Conferences'. These conferences brought together groups of scientists, biologists, mathematicians and anthropologists who were all examining the implications for their own particular fields of the new ideas of systems theory, cybernetics and new theories of communication and information which were just emerging (Lipsett, 1980). Notions of feedback, interrelatedness, the importance of context and circularity were developed at these conferences, and they were later to become very significant concepts in family therapy.

In 1952, Bateson brought these ideas with him when he set up a research project at Palo Alto in California with a number of colleagues, including Jay Haley and John Weakland, to investigate the nature of paradoxes in communication. They began to investigate the processes of communication between patients diagnosed as schizophrenic and their families, and in 1956 they published *Towards a Theory of Schizophrenia* (Bateson et al., 1956). In this paper, they proposed the concept of the 'double bind' as an explanation of schizophrenic behaviour which marked a radical shift from a medical model of schizophrenia as individual pathology to one which located the source of the person's behaviour in the patterns of communication and interaction between family members.

The double-bind hypothesis suggested that the messages people receive have meaning only by virtue of their context, so that if the context of the message contradicts the message itself then people are placed in a double bind. For example, if a father says to his child 'I love you' at the same time as he is hitting the child, the child is placed in a dilemma, a 'bind': the child has to try to make sense of two contradictory messages. However, if the father also insists that the child must not complain or protest about being hit or they will suffer further punishment, the child is placed in a 'double bind': the child must attempt to respond to both messages and must not object to, or comment upon, the contradiction between them. Also, for a person in a very important and dependent relationship, such as that between a child and their father, it is not possible to avoid the double bind by leaving the relationship.

It was the group's hypothesis that much communication in schizophrenic families was like this, and therefore a context was created in which so-called 'schizophrenic behaviour' was the only option available. They suggested that the schizophrenic patient '*must live in a universe where the sequences of events are such that his unconventional communicational habits will in some sense be appropriate*' (original emphasis, Bateson, 1973, p. 177). The shift in thinking involved in this hypothesis was the idea that schizophrenic behaviour was not an irrational response to an illness: it 'made sense' in the context in which it took place. This emphasis on behaviour making sense in context is fundamental to family therapy.

It was this linking of the new communicational approach to schizophrenia, and so to therapy generally, that created the framework for psychiatry to adopt systemic ideas. A number of psychiatrists started to use the Palo Alto group's research ideas in their practice (Ackerman, 1958, 1966; Lidz et al., 1965; Minuchin et al., 1967; Whitaker, 1967; Wynne, 1965) and moved to seeing the whole family together rather than just the individual patient. It was the coming together of new ideas and new practices that gave the initial impetus to the development of family therapy.

However, this was a double-edged development. Although a new way of thinking was introduced into therapy, the ideas became closely linked with a medical/psychiatric approach and were mainly restricted to therapeutic work with families. For this reason, the main schools of family therapy have generally been developed by psychiatrists and in clinical settings: for example, structural family therapy (Minuchin, 1974), the Milan model (Palazzoli et al., 1980) and strategic therapy (Haley, 1976; Madanes, 1981, 1984). Systemic ideas developed by Bateson and his colleagues in a much broader context have been restricted to the relatively narrow fields of therapy with families. It is interesting to note that those practitioners who did use systemic ideas in a more creative and experimental way, such as MacGregor (MacGregor, 1962; MacGregor et al., 1964), who worked with multiple-family groups simultaneously, and Speck and Attneave (1971, 1973), who involved extended family members, neighbours and the wider community in therapy sessions of 50 or 60 people, have had little lasting impact.

The result of this is that today family therapy is regarded within the broad field of social work and by others who work with social problems as a specialist form of practice, usually carried out in psychiatric settings and specialist agencies. It has come to be regarded as an elitist form of therapy which cannot be applied usefully to social care work in general.

Efforts have been made to look at the practical application of family therapy and systemic ideas to the general field of social work and work with social need (Coulshed and Abdulleh-Zadeh, 1983; Dimmock and Dungworth, 1983; Treacher and Carpenter, 1984; Bell et al., 1985; Dale et al., 1986; Kearney, 1986; Evans, 1987c). But although many workers in other settings will have heard of family therapy and are familiar with some of the models of practice, systemic ideas have been slow to reach areas of work outside direct interventions with families. As Jordan has said, there is an 'apparent gap between the evident devotion and enthusiasm for the method among many social workers, and the relatively narrow band of families who receive family therapy . . . [and] . . . above all it has had no apparent influence on the direction of policy in relation to statutory work with families' (Jordan, 1981, p. 269).

As with the unitary approach, many criticisms have been made of family therapy, and for many of the same reasons. These have included the view that it has merely moved the site of pathology from the individual to the family (Jordan, 1981; Treacher, 1986); another criticism is that although family therapists have paid great attention to some family contexts, they have often ignored not only the family's wider context, such as their finances, housing and employment issues, but also the work context of the therapists themselves (Kingston, 1979). Many critics have pointed out that the neutral and relativistic stance of family therapy excludes consideration of issues of power and social context (Taggart, 1985; James and McIntyre, 1983; Erickson, 1988). MacKinnon and Miller (1987) question how far it is possible for therapists to remain 'neutral'. They say that therapists always make choices 'to remain silent, to interpret, to ask certain questions' (p. 148) which have an influence on those they work with. They argue that the risk is ever-present that the therapy will mirror the service users' oppression within society.

Feminist writers in particular have shown how family therapy has adopted a gender-blind approach and encouraged the oppression of women. Goldner (1985, 1988) and Hare-Mustin (1987) criticise family therapy for making issues of gender invisible and unproblematic, thus allowing gender inequalities to remain unchallenged in families, while Luepnitz (1988) and Walters (1990) present strongly critical analyses of the conservative nature of the male-dominated schools of family therapy and the ways in which they maintain relationships which are oppressive to women. In the area of child abuse, feminist writers have attacked family therapy for blaming women for problems in families and underplaying men's responsibility for violence and abuse (MacLeod and Sagara, 1988; Miller, 1990; Langan, 1992).

Issues of race and culture have arguably been even less visible than gender inequality in mainstream family therapy, despite the fact that, at least in the USA, a considerable proportion of those receiving family therapy are black. O'Brien (1990) highlights the fact that two of the early pioneers of the family therapy field (Minuchin and Montalvo, 1971), although writing about severely disadvantaged and mainly black families, paid little attention to the impact of these wider factors on the problems the families were experiencing. In the UK, the implications of a black and Asian perspective for work with families is slowly beginning to emerge (Lau, 1984; Hodes, 1985; O'Brien, 1990).

The balance of power between worker and service user has also received attention, with a number of writers criticising family therapy for using mystifying techniques, excessive jargon and for manipulating families without their consent (Whan, 1983; Treacher, 1988). Similarly, it has been taken to task for disempowering families by using professional power to define the family's problem rather than listening to the family's own definition of the help they need (Howe, 1989; Carpenter, 1992; Reimers and Treacher, 1995).

A systemic approach

As described above, systemic ideas have, in a variety of forms, had some influence in social care work over the last twenty-five years, particularly via the unitary approach and models of family therapy. However, for the reasons we have described, this influence has been quite limited and restricted mainly to more specialist areas of practice. In our view, these constraints are not intrinsic to systemic ideas but rather are related to the contexts in which they have been used – the unitary approach with its background in functionalism and emphasis on consensus, and family therapy with its focus on 'families' and 'therapy' and its close identification with specialist, clinical settings.

Although in outlining a 'systemic approach' we are quite clearly drawing on ideas that have been used in other fields, our aim is to try to distil the key principles of such an approach in a way that makes them available to workers in a wide range of social care contexts. Therefore, we wish to both decontextualise systemic ideas by separating them from the contexts with which they have been identified to date and at the same time attempt to recontextualise them so that they can be made useful in many different settings.

Characteristics of a systemic approach

In common with the other approaches mentioned so far, we believe the key concepts that emerged from the broad shift in 'world view' that took place in the 1940s and 1950s are important for a wide range of disciplines and are particularly useful in social care work. This shift to an approach which emphasises interaction and interdependence rather than individual and isolated responses offers a way of understanding how social need arises and how we can intervene to meet it.

Figure 2.1 shows a simplified way to identify the shift in thinking from a 'traditional' paradigm to a systemic one. The column on the left in Figure 2.1 outlines some of the characteristics of what might be called a 'traditional' approach to social casework and therapy of the pre-generalist era, to use Barber's (1991) phrase. There is an emphasis on one person who has professional knowledge and expertise acting on other individuals ('clients') who are passive recipients of these actions. The professional worker is seen as separate from outside influences and solely responsible for their own actions. The basis of their work is a one-to-one relationship in which the worker acts on behalf of, or for, the 'client'. The direction of the influence is one-way: from the worker to the client.

Traditional	Systemic
Action	Interaction
Individual	Relationship
Isolated	In context
One-person unit	More than one-person unit
Unidirectional influence	Reciprocal influence
Content	Process
Event	Pattern
Random	Structure
Reductionist	Integrative/holistic

Figure 2.1   Traditional versus systemic paradigms

This focus leads to an approach based on activity and content: what and how much has been done. Even 'event', whether it is a visit or a meeting or a telephone call, is seen as separate and unrelated. The activities often develop in reactive fashion as workers respond to each individual request made to them.

The key aspect is that events or activities are seen in isolation and separate from each other, so there is no clear overall framework that links them together. This means that 'clients' and their problems are reduced to specific problems – a family needs their electricity bill paid; a single person has nowhere to live; a child has been bruised. Figure 2.2 illustrates the position of the worker from this perspective.

On the other hand, a systemic approach emphasises relationships, context, mutual influence and pattern. The basis of this approach is that it always considers the context in which any actions take place. It operates in the belief that everyone, whether service user or worker, is influenced by the contexts in which they live and work. Therefore, individuals are always seen as part of larger contexts, and they both influence and are influenced by these contexts.

From a systemic perspective, all of us can be seen as operating within multiple contexts simultaneously. We work within organisations and agencies with duties and responsibilities, and many of these limit and constrain what actions we can take in a particular situation. Similarly, all the people we come in contact with are operating within a wide range of contexts which

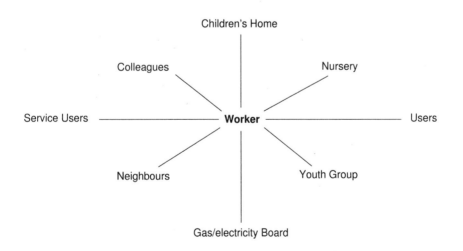

Figure 2.2   A worker's contact with service users, agencies and other groups: A traditional model

both limit and influence their requests and responses. They may be involved in the local community or club. Schools and work settings will be of importance. Within all these contexts, the influence of the social worker may be very small. Figure 2.3 outlines this context for a local authority worker.

Figure 2.3   A systemic model

In any situation, workers always bring with them beliefs, values, assumptions and prejudices which will affect the way they interact with those they meet. Workers need to be very conscious that they are not objective onlookers: their presence affects people's responses. Therefore, any worker using a systemic approach should always be conscious that there is a wider picture, and so they need to take an integrated rather than reductionist view. It is necessary to look for the pattern and structure in a series of events rather than concentrate on the events in isolation.

We see this approach as a means of making sense of workers' involvement, because it places the activities in a wider context and examines the effects of the interactions themselves rather than the results of specific actions.

A systemic approach and issues of power

From an interactional perspective, the process of the relationship between the worker and service user, as well as the outcome of the interaction, is of vital importance. However, such relationships do not take place in a vacuum, and they are always constrained by the relative power balance between them.

We have outlined above the many critiques which claim that systems theory, the unitary approach and family therapy have excluded consideration of race, gender, class, sexual orientation and disability, as well as the question of professional power. However, this could only be done by ignoring key aspects of the wider context influencing any system. In any human system, it makes a great difference to the interaction between the people within the system whether they are all of the same cultural background or of different cultural backgrounds; whether they are all one gender or different genders; whether they are all able-bodied or are a mix of able-bodied and disabled people, and whether they are all middle-class or are from all classes of society. Such differences of race, gender, class and ability will have an effect on the power relationships between the members in any system. (Other differences in power are explored in detail in Chapter 4.)

This 'power blindness' led some family therapists to argue that in an abusive family, both the man who committed the abuse and the woman or child who were abused were equally responsible for the abuse occurring. This view reached its pinnacle with the statement by one of the leading theorists of family therapy in the 1980s, Humberto Maturana, who, when asked about the notion of power, said: 'Power is created by submission' (quoted in MacKinnon and Miller, 1987). Such a view is similar to saying that people who abuse power are 'forced' to do so because someone has 'submitted' to them: a completely untenable position which is at odds with the day-to-day experience both of social workers and service users.

We believe that if the importance of context is properly recognised, then an analysis of the power relationships within and between systems is essential. This is particularly true if social need is to be alleviated to any degree by changes in the social order. Therefore, power relationships have to be regarded as one of the essential aspects of the context in which social need is both maintained and resolved.

We suggest that, as a framework for understanding relationships between people, systemic ideas are valid and useful, but they are not sufficient. As relationships between people – human systems – always involve power issues, it is necessary for workers to be able to understand and work with these power issues, as well as to think systemically.

It is our view that in any interactional process, both workers and service users bring to the relationship their beliefs, values, prejudices, experiences and a range of theoretical ideas and understandings. These then provide the context for the interactions between the two parties.

Drawing on feminist values, McNay (1992) likewise attempts to integrate systems theory and power relations in order to help social workers develop an empowering mode of intervention. She argues that:

> Systems theory can be applied to any society, regardless of its particular norms or values, since it describes an interaction process. It is particular theories which pro-vide the analysis of the society and which are underpinned by particular values and theoretical perspective which may explain social interaction in terms of con-sensus or conflict. (McNay, 1992, p. 57)

Whether a systemic approach is radical or conservative depends on the values which the worker brings to the relationship. As Leonard (1975) and Evans (1976) claimed, the systems theory of the time was criticised as con-servative because those who used it were operating from a conservative view of society. MacKinnon and Miller (1987) make the same point in relation to the Milan model of family therapy, saying that while the approach 'may have greater potential to incorporate a radical analysis than has any earlier family therapy paradigm, in practice, the approach seems constrained by the sociopolitical conservatism of its proponents' (p. 153).

Once a distinction is made between systemic ideas and the values with which they have been applied, it becomes possible to consider how they might be linked in a more critical and radical approach.

Over the last thirty years, a range of such critical approaches have been developed from the radical social work of the 1960s and early 1970s (Bailey and Brake, 1975) through feminist practice (Brook and Davis, 1985; Hanmer and Statham, 1988; Dominelli and McLeod, 1989) and anti-racist practice (Ely and Denney, 1987; Dominelli, 1988) to the models of anti-discriminatory and anti-oppressive practice which are currently emerging (Langan and Day, 1992; Thompson, 1993).

During this period, some limited efforts have been made to attempt to link a systemic approach with these radical ideas. As mentioned above, Leonard (1975) felt that systems theory could benefit a radical approach to social work. Although feminist writers have differing views on whether family therapy and feminist approaches can be linked, some have suggested ways in which the two can be used positively to challenge traditional views of women's position in families (Osborne, 1983; Pilalis and Anderton, 1986). Ahmad (1992), as discussed above, suggested ideas for linking the unitary approach and a black perspective, and O'Brien (1990) gives some useful guidelines for conducting family therapy with black families. However, these efforts to link radical ideas and an interactional approach have had a limited impact on practice.

Although we wish to promote the shift in thinking that is contained in the systemic ideas outlined above, we do not take on board the limitations to practice implied by the application of these ideas within a framework of family therapy, psychiatry or the unitary model. We feel that the ideas are not inherently conservative but can be used, in conjunction with critical and radical approaches, to work towards an anti-oppressive and empowering framework for practice.

In the remainder of this book, we will examine and illustrate how such a systemic approach can be applied effectively within a wide range of settings by people working in social care.

3 Key principles of a systemic approach

The main emphasis of this book is on using a systemic approach in a wide range of different settings and contexts. We have put forward the view that its value lies in offering a broad framework: not only for understanding and analysing many of the situations and problems people are faced with in their day-to-day work, but also as a method of deciding on the most suitable means of intervening in them to achieve effective change. In this chapter, we outline what we see as the key principles of a systemic approach, and we illustrate by example the implications of applying these principles in practice.

These principles are based on the key ideas which emerged from the shift in thinking described in Chapter 2. They are not limited to particular professions or work settings, and they do not require that the practitioner abide by a specific model of practice or use specialist techniques. However, they do provide a framework for workers to structure and plan their work, and they are a means of facilitating the use of workers' existing skills.

Although the main focus of this chapter is on approaches to practice that are useful to practitioners in thinking about their work, it is very important that such ideas are used within a context which pays full attention to the wishes and rights of service users. Much of the dissatisfaction with models of family therapy, where a number of these ideas have been used most extensively, results from the ways in which they were used to emphasise the therapist's power and render users 'invisible' (Reimers and Treacher, 1995).

As with any practice model, aspects of the service users' context – such as cultural background, gender, religion, age and sexual orientation – need to be acknowledged and respected as part of a worker's fundamental value position. Basic principles like informed consent, confidentiality and service user autonomy underpin any forms of practice and are equally as important when using the principles suggested here. We see these key principles as:

- maintaining consistency;
- recognising the importance of context;
- taking a positive approach;
- identifying patterns of behaviour;
- emphasising process;
- working with others.

Maintaining consistency

In order to apply a systemic approach successfully, it is advisable to adopt this approach consistently within all the contexts of work. It is important to emphasise that adopting such a perspective does involve a shift in world view. It is not possible to hold on to an individualistic and reductionist model of human relationships while applying a systemic approach: at a basic level, the two positions are incompatible.

However, this does not mean that it is impossible to understand and to utilise a variety of theoretical approaches. It is certainly possible, for instance, to combine some insights offered by a psychodynamic framework with a systemic approach in working in a given situation.

One question people often ask about the approach is: 'Is it possible to work with just one individual using a systemic approach?' The answer to this is always 'Yes', as every person is part of a network of relationships with families, friends, neighbours, communities and organisations, which create the living context of that person. Therefore, although the worker's work setting may require a focus on the individual service user, the worker can consider the service user's wider context, and thus the choice of intervention can be influenced by the worker's theoretical approach.

On the other hand, a psychodynamically-orientated worker may decide to see a whole family together, but their choice of intervention is still likely to be informed by their individualistic framework.

A specific example of the need for consistency from a systemic perspective was the public outcry over the action of the social work department and police in Orkney in 1990, when a group of children were removed from their homes in what were described in the press as 'dawn raids'. The issue in this case was not whether social services were right or wrong in their action or whether it was necessary to remove the children from their beds at dawn, it was rather that, having had the experience of the controversies caused by similar action in Cleveland and Rochdale, the social work department did not prepare itself in advance to answer the criticisms this action would inevitably receive from the press and general public.

We are not commenting here on whether the social work department deserved criticism for their actions, but we would certainly argue that the department deserved criticism for ignoring a crucial aspect of context and for not anticipating the response their actions would generate.

The application of the systemic approach does not begin when some action takes place, nor is it related to one specific person or group. It needs to be applied all the time to all the contexts in which the worker is involved. Workers using the approach are always asking themselves the questions:

> *In which contexts am I operating?*
> *What are the opportunities and constraints that they offer?*
> *What is the aim of my involvement?*
> *What powers and responsibilities have I?*
> *What are the likely effects of my interventions?*

The answers to some or all of these questions will change or become more or less important as the workers receive feedback in response to their actions.

Field social workers receiving a referral will on the one hand ask themselves:

> *What is the meaning of the information I have been given here?*
> *Is the person who has requested a bath aid actually looking for more than that?*
> *What action must be taken now, and what needs further thought or consultation?*

On the other hand, they will also ask themselves:

> *What is my role here?*
> *What are my powers and responsibilities?*
> *What resources are available?*
> *Am I the best person to respond to this request?*
> *What are the implications of responding to this request?*

A local authority community development worker preparing for a meeting with local councillors on behalf of a group of local residents needs to ask very carefully: 'What is my role here? Who am I accountable to?' A worker in a residential home for children needs to constantly ask the question: 'What is the child attempting to communicate through his/her behaviour? What will be the effect if I respond in this way?'

Recognising the importance of context

Recognition of context is one of the most important aspects of a systemic approach. It is the framework of people and organisations, events, thoughts, and beliefs which surround all of us every day. We live and work in multiple contexts and move from one to another all the time. We are essentially part of our context, which means that we are not only influenced by it, we also influence it at the same time. This has considerable implications for how we explain behaviour, whether that of people or organisations, as a shift of context can take place very quickly without our noticing it is happening.

In order to guide our behaviour in different situations, we all rely on what are called 'context markers' (Bateson, 1973). These are pieces of information which tell us the context we are operating in at any one time. For example, if we see a group of men attacking another man in the street, we would probably feel we should call the police or take some other action to help the person being attacked. However, if we see the same scene but are at the time in our local theatre watching a performance of *Julius Caesar* by William Shakespeare, calling the police would probably not be appreciated by the rest of the audience.

Much of the work carried out by Gregory Bateson and his colleagues described in Chapter 2 involved examining the importance of context markers, particularly in work with people diagnosed as schizophrenic. They postulated that such people, because of the circumstances they find themselves in, leave out context markers, so that when a person diagnosed as schizophrenic says they are 'Jesus Christ' or 'Hitler', it is not possible for the listener to clarify whether they are being serious, joking or have been offered a part in a play.

When working with people, it is always important to clarify the context at the initial stage of the contact. Workers should establish the context markers and state clearly the nature of the relationship between themselves and the individual or family. If, for example, it is an interview taking place in the agency office, the worker should make clear the purpose and function of the agency and what its responsibilities are. If the worker is a duty social worker who meets with service users when they first call in at the office and who then refers them on to another worker or agency, the worker should explain this role before the person goes into great detail about what may be difficult and upsetting experiences if that is not necessary for the purpose of the interview.

The clarification of context is particularly important when power issues are involved and there may be a possibility of some legal or formal action taking place that might affect the service user, either now or in the future. In the case of a probation officer, it is essential to indicate that the relationship between the worker and the offender cannot be a confidential one, because there is also a legal contract laid down by the court. Therefore, if the offender gives the probation officer information concerning illegal activities, that information cannot be regarded as confidential within their relationship. Because of the legal context, the officer would have to consider taking appropriate action whether the offender agreed or not.

The possibility of confusion about context often arises in child care work, when the initial contact between the family and the agency occurs because the family are looking for help. The worker and the family start to build up a voluntary helping relationship, and the parents come to trust the worker. However, if an allegation is then made that the children are at risk and the agency takes action against the parents' wishes, parents can feel great resentment that their request for help has been turned against them. In other words, the family's original approach to the agency is based on the belief that the context is one of the agency providing help for them. If it is not made clear that the agency also has a statutory role which can change the context, it is very likely that problems will arise.

Similarly, voluntary workers often work in situations where it is very important that their responsibility, a key aspect of context, is clear. They are often asked to work on a one-to-one level with mothers or young people, and they are encouraged to build up close and supportive relationships with them. However, if as a result of this relationship the service user shares with them some information concerning illegal activities or child abuse, the volunteer can feel that their relationship with the family is compromised. For this reason, it is vital that such relationships and responsibilities are sorted out beforehand.

It is clear from these examples that as well as behaviour being defined by the context, it is also a circular process, and we as workers play a large part in creating our own contexts by the way we behave. Therefore, workers must always be conscious of the ways in which they influence contexts – the context markers they put down.

One of the omissions of more traditional forms of practice which concentrate on the individual (or the family) is that the wider agency context is excluded and ignored. This limited view can operate at any level. It might be that the worker does not make clear to the service user the worker's role and function within the agency, as in the examples above, or that the agency as a whole does not clarify and check on what policies it wishes carried out and how they are to be implemented. The 'pin-down' scandal in Staffordshire (Utting Report, 1992) is a good example of the latter failing. Here staff were successful in controlling children and stopping them absconding, but only by using completely unacceptable means, such as taking their clothes away for long periods, treating teenagers as very young children, and locking them up in rooms for days on end.

Wider still, there is the social, economic and political context that effects everyone, such as cuts in public spending. These mean that services and benefits are reduced, which makes it harder for families to care for their children and for old people to find proper residential accommodation. Factors such as unemployment, poor housing and poverty are also part of the wider context in which many clients live, and issues of race, gender, class and sexual orientation also create contexts which affect service users.

The importance of recognising the wider social context is well illustrated by research which indicates that many more women experience mental health problems than men (Mollica and Mills, 1986; Ussher, 1991), that there are proportionally many more black children in care than white (CRE, 1977) and that proportionally more black people than white are compulsorily admitted to hospital (Frederick, 1991; Burke, 1986; Fernando, 1991).

Unfortunately, workers and agencies often take a very limited view, and only certain contexts are considered. While it has been a consistent finding of the reports into child abuse scandals that what is needed is more training for staff (Blom-Cooper, 1985, 1988; Utting Report, 1992), very little attention has been paid to wider issues, such as poor housing, poverty and unemployment, in understanding why the abuse took place, or to the lack of resources for social work as a reason why the child was not protected (Parton, 1985). The report into the Staffordshire residential care scandal recommended that there needed to be more training for residential managers, not that there should be better pay and conditions for staff (Utting Report, 1992).

One example of the importance of considering the wider context is the case of Jasmine Beckford, a young girl who was killed by her stepfather, despite considerable long-term input from the social services department. One of the supposed mysteries of the case was why the social worker had only seen Jasmine on one occasion, despite visiting the family 56 times. On one level, this seems incredible and extremely bad practice, and the judge in the case described the social worker as 'naive beyond belief' (Blom-Cooper, 1985). The explanation offered at the time was that the social worker's training and beliefs led her to believe that concentrating on the mother rather than the child was the appropriate approach. However, the difficulty with this explanation is that it does not explain why the social worker was judged to have carried out reasonable work on similar cases. The explanation is also very individually-focused, concentrating on the actions of the individual worker and practice.

However, a wider view offers a different explanation for the worker's behaviour. In the Beckford case, the social worker was a white woman, while the stepfather who killed Jasmine was a black man, reported to have a history of violence. In this context, the issues of gender, race and violence could all be considered as playing a part in affecting the social worker's behaviour. It is quite possible that she had some anxiety, as a woman, about working with and possibly having to confront a potentially violent man. As a white person, she may have had some stereotypical attitudes to working with a black person where violence is possibly an issue. She may also have wished to support another woman, Jasmine's mother, if she felt she was being abused by her partner. All or some of these possibilities would offer a coherent explanation which would help make sense of why the worker would want to concentrate her efforts on the mother and at the same time wish to avoid any confrontation with her black, male partner over the child.

From a systemic perspective, we always need to consider the wider context in order to help us make sense of what seems at first hand to be unexplained behaviour.

Adopting a positive approach

Work in social care involves constant exposure to all kinds of personal difficulties, with their associated misery, unhappiness and stress. It is not surprising, therefore, that workers often develop a problem-orientated attitude, not only towards those they work with but very often towards their colleagues and their organisations as well. As we discussed in Chapter 1, the whole notion of 'problems' and 'problem-solving' has this disadvantage. It can lead to an overemphasis on people's deficiencies and inadequacies, with little recognition of their positive attributes. We wish to take a different position and view social work, social care and the other helping professions in a positive light, as we feel that they have a necessary and valuable role to play in society.

We believe that the staff in residential homes for old people do make the lives of the residents more rewarding, that community care can provide a valuable and useful service, that youth workers do help young people make decisions about their futures, that social workers do provide an important service in protecting children and that community workers can help groups and communities take more power over the decisions that effect them.

However, this positive view is not based on some naive 'rule of optimism', as Blom-Cooper (1985) described the position of the social workers in the Jasmine Beckford case. We are only too aware of the tragedies that have taken place: the deaths of children such as Jasmine Beckford, Kimberley Carlile and Maria Colwell, to mention only the most familiar cases; the deaths of older people left alone in their homes, and the suffering of children and other people in residential care. There have also been the criticisms of social workers and their practice in the child sexual abuse controversies of Cleveland, Rochdale and Orkney, and of their 'political correctness' in aspects of anti-oppressive practice. No doubt, readers can think of other examples of tragedies, scandals and inquiries that have beset social care in the last decade or so.

We recognise that there have been grounds to criticise the practice of workers and their managers in many of these cases, but in reality, these examples only make up a small proportion of the thousands of tasks undertaken by workers in personal social services every day of the week.

Moreover, it is clear that these scandals have had their effect, both on the public image of social work and the morale of those working in social services agencies. We would agree with Preston-Shoot and Agass (1990) that a negative spiral has developed, where the poor public image, combined with lack of resources and more demands, has made workers and agencies defensive, with the result that there is a concentration on the negative aspects of work with service users, and more positive aspects are ignored. The spate of public inquiries has led to increased efforts to exercise greater control over what workers in the personal social services do, by producing more guidelines and regulations.

A similar process can be observed in some workers' attitudes to service users when viewing them in a negative light as 'demanding', 'inadequate', 'resistant' or 'manipulative'. From a systemic perspective, these views are one-sided and limited. They do not take into account the role of the worker or the agency in helping to 'construct' these responses by the service users. In many cases, the service users' so-called 'aggression' is a logical response to trying to deal with a system that cannot provide the help they need. Such attitudes can lead to negative spirals which are de-skilling and unhelpful to both service user and worker.

Therefore, one key principle of the approach is to recognise competence rather than inadequacy, positives as well as problems. This is not a call to deny the very real problems and difficulties people have to deal with in their lives, but rather an acknowledgement that people are not just their 'problems': they also have a wide range of skills and resources which can enable them to deal with these difficulties. This approach is very much an empowering one, aimed at mobilising people's resources.

Every agency has both positive and negative aspects which can be utilised by the workers within it. For example, social services departments have a diverse range of services and responsibilities (NISW, 1982), and there are many points of access where the agency and community intersect. A social services department office is part of a larger network of settings it is possible to gain access to in order to use a wide variety of resources. These can include residential and day care establishments, juvenile justice facilities, clubs and activities for groups such as elderly and disabled people, home helps and family aides, specialist workers, community care schemes, and many more. By using a systemic approach, a worker has the opportunity to intervene in many different ways and utilising a wide range of techniques and approaches.

One technique for implementing a positive approach is called 'reframing' and has been developed by a number of systemic therapists (Haley, 1973; Erickson and Rossi, 1979; Rossi, 1980; De Shazer, 1982; O'Hanlon, 1987). Reframing basically involves helping someone change the way they look at and experience their situation: the context for understanding their situation is changed (Watzlawick et al., 1974). One example would be to say to a single parent who is feeling depressed and incompetent and is describing a long list of problems: 'Despite all the difficulties you are dealing with, you have still managed to get to the interview and are obviously concerned enough about your situation to want to do something about it.' This statement does not attempt to take away the person's problems with some magic solution, but it does start to identify some positive aspects of what is happening and acknowledge right at the start areas of competence which are realistic and fit in with the person's experience.

Identifying patterns of behaviour

The common image of people who work in social care is that they are very rushed, always having too much to do and too little time to do it. It often feels as if one is just moving from crisis to crisis. For many people in this situation, the working day is made up of a series of events, such as telephone calls, visits, interviews, meetings, etc., which are not necessarily carried out in any particular order and have to be squeezed into the spaces in the diary between other planned events. Workers often feel that they are not in control of these events but instead are being pushed along by the tide.

Of course, there are many reasons for this: workers *do* have too much to do and too few resources to do it. But as well as these practical issues, there are other organisational and structural reasons for the feelings of being over-loaded that affect many workers. From a systemic perspective, it is inevitable that if someone works on their own, they will get 'sucked into' the problematic aspects of what they are working with, whether it is a single client, a resident, family or group. This is because, in any situation, a worker will be influenced by as well as influencing the service user.

In this context of being caught up in a continual series of 'events', it is very difficult to remain aware of the wider perspective and to step back enough to observe the patterns that link the events together. An example of this process is provided by a situation where a resident in an elderly person's home was regarded by all the staff as being difficult because he responded with out-bursts of shouting and aggressive language at unpredictable times. Each interaction between the man and different staff members was seen as a separate event. As a result of this, both the staff and other residents became wary of him, and so he was isolated and ignored. This in turn served to exaggerate and increase the original behaviour.

One of the authors, acting as a consultant to the staff group, suggested that for a couple of weeks they should not change how they were managing this resident but instead observe his behaviour, in particular to try to see what other events took place each time he became aggressive. It quickly became clear that his anger occurred when he received letters. When this link was explored, it turned out that the letters that upset him were from his son and daughter-in-law, with whom he had been very close. However, the resident felt his son was writing to him so that he would not have to visit, and he was very unhappy about this. When the staff became aware of what was upsetting the resident, they were able to understand the cause of his anger and to support him.

By moving from responding to specific events of anger to examining the pattern of behaviour that surrounded the events, the staff were able to make sense of the man's behaviour. In interactional terms, the meaning of the event is not in the event itself but in the relationship between it and the context in which it is embedded.

The task of identifying 'the pattern which connects', in Bateson's (1979) phrase, and thus of understanding the meaning for people of behaviour, is a crucial aspect of implementing a systemic approach. Once the pattern is identified, the choice of intervention becomes easier. As a pattern is, by its very nature, made up of the connections between people and events, it is possible to intervene at many different points in order to achieve change. Because the aim is to alter the patterns of behaviour, the method of intervention is not necessarily important; much more important is matching the intervention to the appropriate part of the pattern of behaviour.

Patterns exist at all levels of organisations: one can see patterns in individual's behaviour, in groups, in teams of staff, in large organisations, in political behaviour, etc. From a systemic perspective, all behaviour occurs within patterns, so a structure can be identified as underlying it. Therefore, in trying to understand the situation people are in, one is always looking for pattern and structure.

In working with a young couple who were concerned about the behaviour of their 4-year-old boy, one of the authors was able to observe a clear pattern of behaviour involving all family members. Watching a video tape of a family session, it was possible to see that whenever the mother started to talk about the boy's 'bad' behaviour, the boy would immediately begin to behave badly. He would tease his younger sister and make her scream. His father would not respond to this but would make a joke of the situation. The mother then intervened to control the boy, and as soon as she attempted to do this, the boy would go to his father for support. The situation would then quieten down until the next time the mother criticised the boy's behaviour. In the space of a one-hour session, it was possible to observe this pattern repeated in a variety of different forms at least twenty times. Using this information, the worker was able to intervene in the family pattern and address issues of gender roles and power which were helping to maintain the problem of the child's behaviour.

Another important aspect of pattern is that it also applies to us as workers. If we do not observe our own patterns of behaviour, we can become part of the problem. As we are always part of the relationship that is created with the service users, we have some part in developing patterns of behaviour with them. Dale et al. (1986) give a number of examples illustrating how welfare professionals can play a large part in maintaining situations that place children at risk.

Emphasising process

One of the key differences between a systemic approach and other models of practice is the emphasis given to process. Some workers concentrate on the individual, the *content* of events, and try to find the cause of behaviour. A worker taking a systemic view, however, is much more interested in the relationships, the *context* of events, the patterns underlying it, and the interactional process that takes place on a continual basis. Just as there is an underlying structure that connects particular events or people – the *pattern* – there are also the continual interactions which are taking place within all the relationships – the *process*.

In any interaction between people, the process is often as important as the content, if not more so. The importance of process in relation to content is encapsulated in the phrase 'It's not what you do, it's the way that you do it.' The relationship between process and content has been described in terms of chewing gum: if you are chewing gum, the gum is the content and the chewing is the process (Doyle and Straus, 1976). The useful thing about this analogy is that it is easy to see that if the content is changed from gum to toffee, the process remains the same.

This is particularly important in working within the areas of equal opportunities and empowerment. If the process is not right, no matter how much the content is changed – from questions of access to user involvement, to training, to equal opportunities in jobs – the issue will still not be resolved.

One important process in implementing an equal opportunities policy concerns addressing the problem of involving those who are going to be affected by the policy in planning and organising it. This issue has been taken up more seriously in recent legislation aimed at involving people in the consultation process around community care plans and the involvement of parents under the new Children Act (1989). Traditional social work values, such as respect, autonomy and self-determination, are examples of process issues – how people are treated.

Many of the difficulties that arise in working with people in social care result from insufficient attention being paid to the process of interaction between the people involved. The large number of bulging case files in personal social services agencies all over the UK shows that accumulating more 'content' in the form of detailed information does not necessarily mean improved practice. In human relationships, there will always be more content than can be gathered and analysed. By identifying the patterns of behaviour which structure the content, it is possible to reveal the processes which underpin the difficulties.

One important aspect of process concerns the need to clarify the relationship between the worker and the service user. It is something which needs to be addressed continually by everyone involved in working with people. As well as the straightforward aspects – such as clarifying the purpose of meetings, interviews, conferences, letters and telephone calls, and defining the role and responsibilities of the people present – there are also more subtle aspects of maintaining clarity. These include using feedback during the course of a conversation to make sure that what was clear at the beginning continues to be clear; always checking out changes in context – for example, what may have happened to the person since the last meeting; summarising decisions and agreements at regular intervals; checking that everyone involved in a situation – partners, parents and children, agency and service user – is clear about what is taking place.

The following example illustrates how process issues can affect the interaction between a worker and service users. A worker was seeing a married couple who had referred themselves to a counselling agency. Very little information was provided by the initial referral, which was made by the woman over the telephone. All that the referral said was that she, the wife, was unhappy with her relationship with her husband as he was staying out of the house a good deal, sometimes until late at night, and was being very secretive about money. The person taking the call asked the woman if she would ask her husband to come along with her. The woman said she would but was doubtful that he would come.

This particular agency used a live consultancy model in its work, where the worker meets with the service users in one room, and colleagues acting as consultants observe the session by video in a different room. Prior to the session, the worker and his colleagues discussed ideas around the referral as a means of planning and structuring the process of the interview. One hypothesis was that the husband might be involved with another woman, as he was said to be out a good deal, including late at night, and appeared to be spending a lot of money. At this stage, not having met the couple, these ideas were only speculation and could be abandoned straight away if they turned out to be inaccurate.

The worker then met the couple, and the session began well enough. The woman began to say what she felt the problems with her husband were. She said he stayed out late, would not talk to her or say where he had been, and he spent money without consulting her. She kept asking him what he was doing and where he went, and he argued back, saying that he did not go any-where, and anyway, he had a right to do what he wanted. This discussion quickly escalated into an argument which went round and round, with neither person willing to shift their position. The more the argument con-tinued, the more it seemed likely that there was some truth in the hypothesis that the husband might be involved in another relationship.

However, observing from the outside, it was very noticeable that the more the couple argued the more the worker withdrew from the situation, and the more he withdrew the more the couple argued. After a short while, the worker had become completely silent, and the couple were left arguing with each other. It was clear that the worker was not in control of the situation; also, by not saying anything, he was allowing the unhelpful pattern of inter-action between the couple to continue. This did not help in trying to identify positive areas of competence in their relationship.

At that point, a consultation break was taken, and the worker came out of the session to discuss what was happening. The worker's explanation of what he experienced in the room is an interesting example of the power of the interactional process to 'suck' the worker into it. The worker said that as the session progressed, he became conscious that the original hypothesis the team had suggested before the session might be correct – that the husband was having an affair. However, he had no idea what to do if this fact emerged in the session itself, and therefore he became immobilised and unable to think clearly. Because of this, he lost control of the therapeutic process of the session and began to feel powerless as the couple continued arguing. In fact, he had become stuck in the process of the interactions with the couple and had started to take responsibility for their problem, rather than concentrating on being responsible for the session and letting the couple be responsible for their situation.

After the discussion with his colleagues, the worker went back into the interview and took control of the session by agreeing some clear ground rules: only one person should talk at a time and each person should have equal time to put their point of view; he also reached agreement with the couple that their relationship could be discussed in the session. He then asked each person to clarify, from their point of view, what the problem was for each of them. These actions enabled him to explore the interactional process which had become 'stuck'. In the ensuing discussion, the wife was then able to say she was suspicious that her husband was having an affair, and he then admitted that he was. The work with the couple continued into helping them decide where their relationship would go from there.

In this example, the problem was not that the worker was incompetent or that the couple were being 'resistant'. However, the worker had been 'sucked into' the couple's relationship, which meant that the process between the three of them itself became stuck. As a result, he was not able to facilitate a helpful interaction between the wife and husband.

Working with others

So far, we have given great emphasis in this book to the importance of considering context and reciprocal influence in working in social care, and we have illustrated some of the practical difficulties that arise when these aspects of a systemic approach are not recognised. However, from our point of view, possibly the most critical implication of utilising a systemic approach is the effect it has on the way people work.

In traditional models of practice, the approach to service users is very much by an individual worker, and the style of the worker is likewise very individualistic. The worker is seen as making independent and objective judgements about the people they are working with. This individualistic model of practice is one of the reasons why Pithouse says that social work is an 'invisible trade'. He argues that:

> Social work is invisible in three particular ways. First, social workers who visit people in the privacy of their own homes or see them in the office usually do so *free from observation and interference by their colleagues* [my emphasis], who likewise pursue a similar form of intervention. Secondly . . . [it] is invisible to the extent that the outcomes of interventions are uncertain and ambiguous . . . Thirdly, social work is invisible in so far as practitioners do not typically retrieve and analyse the occupational processes that surround their endeavours. (Pithouse, 1987, p. 2)

He suggests that because of these three invisible aspects of social work, it is 'in the organisational setting that sense is made of practice; it is here that work is "seen" and understood' (Pithouse, 1987, p. 3). More specifically, it is during one-to-one supervision sessions that the evaluation of unobserved practice occurs, and the 'invisibility of encounters with consumers and the outcomes of these unobserved events is rendered satisfactory or otherwise within the supervisory relationship' (Pithouse, 1987, p. 8). He argues that social work interactions are actually constructed on the basis of the worker's reports to their supervisor: no one else sees the interaction with the service user, certainly not in field or clinical settings.

On the other hand, from the theoretical perspective of a systemic approach, the position of the worker is very different. As soon as a worker makes any contact, whether it is with an individual service user, a family, a group, or another organisation, by whatever means – telephone, letter, home visit, office interview – they are immediately both influencing this new interaction and being influenced by it. The worker then becomes a part of a new interaction between the service user or organisation and themselves. As a result, it is not possible for the worker to have a completely neutral and objective stance. We have already described situations where workers get 'sucked into' the relationships they are working within and often become part of the problem for the service user – by maintaining them as dependent, incompetent or powerless – rather than part of the solution.

In order to try to work with this interactional process, it is useful to create another relationship which will allow workers to achieve some distance from the relationship they are involved in. In using the phrase 'joint working', we seek to emphasise an approach where the worker does not work on their own but has at least one other worker commenting on or observing their work.

The most common term used to describe this process is 'consultation', and the word is used in this context to mean that the practitioner is working with colleagues where there is no relationship of accountability between them (Brown, 1984). This means that any discussions which take place are always advisory: one worker cannot instruct the other to do something. In fact, it is quite common for the worker to be observed by colleagues in a number of settings, such as in residential and day care units, health settings, and community and youth work. In such settings, the worker's actions and responses can be readily observed by both colleagues and service users alike. However, it has not generally been the case that those observing have used the opportunity to give constructive feedback in a structured way to the worker involved.

The range of methods to facilitate joint working outlined below have mainly been developed in therapeutic and counselling contexts, but they can easily be adapted for use in any kind of social care setting. The essential point of joint working or consultation from a systemic perspective is that some means is used to obtain another opinion from 'outside' the interactional process between the worker and the service user.

While the methods and techniques described below are presented from the point of view of the worker, it is of course crucial to pay close attention to the position of the service user when considering using any of these methods. Models of live consultation and live supervision impinge directly on the service user's relationship with the worker and should only be used with the informed consent of users. Unfortunately, the use of some of these methods in family therapy and the reliance on specialist equipment such as one-way screens, video cameras and 'ear bugs' – where the supervisor is able to talk directly to the therapist during the meeting with the family – have had an alienating and disempowering effect on families (Howe, 1989; Reimers and Treacher, 1995). It is also likely that dependence on such technology is another reason that family therapy ideas have not been taken on board by the broad field of social care work.

However, the overall process of joint working can offer a range of useful techniques to workers if the key social work values of partnership, respect and confidentiality are applied equally in this context as in any other. In our own practice experience, using a colleague as a 'consultant', in whatever setting the work was taking place, whether it was a family home, a day centre or an office, was very helpful in keeping a clear perspective on our work.

Methods of joint working

Once workers think beyond working in isolation, there is a wide range of ways to work jointly with colleagues. Many of these methods will be familiar, but the key difference is in the thinking that lies behind their use. To work with colleagues effectively does not require that those colleagues have specialist skills or experience, but rather that they are outside the interactional process between the worker and the service user, as illustrated in Figure 3.1.

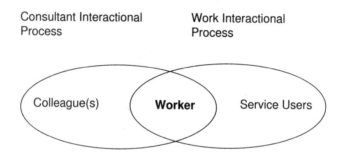

Figure 3.1   A systemic model of joint working

There is a wide range of literature describing the variety of techniques and models of joint working that can be used to achieve this position 'outside' the interactional process (Carpenter, 1984; Cornwall and Pearson, 1981; Evans, 1987a; Haley, 1976; Kingston and Smith, 1983; Liddle and Halpin, 1978; Liddle et al., 1988; Montalvo, 1973; Olsen and Pegg, 1979). There is also no restriction on the type of colleague who can act as a consultant. As practitioners, both authors have used a wide range of colleagues as consultants to their work. These people have included social work colleagues, residential staff, community nurses, medical staff and students, and we have always found the outside view of these people to be helpful in planning our interventions.

Some of the main methods of joint working that we have found useful are:

- discussions with individual colleagues;
- group discussions;
- discussions of 'options';

- pre- and post-work planning with colleagues;
- roleplay/sculpting;
- live consultation;
- use of video/audio facilities;
- 'time out'/self-consultation.

Discussions with individual colleagues

Most people who work in personal social service agencies spend a considerable amount of time discussing their work with colleagues. Sometimes, these discussions are little more than gossiping or complaining sessions. While this may be a useful release of frustration, it is rarely helpful for the work itself.

A simple way to use colleagues as consultants on a piece of work is to structure this informal discussion time and ask colleagues specific questions about the issues of concern. A good way to structure such a discussion is to draw a rough 'eco-map' of the case in question, so that they have a visual image of the people involved and the relationships between them. We have often found that a brief, structured discussion of about 15 minutes can be sufficient to identify the pattern of interaction that is blocking our progress in a piece of work.

Group discussions

Many work teams hold regular group meetings to discuss various matters, including policies and procedures. It is quite easy, therefore, to ask the team for advice about specific work difficulties using the structured procedure outlined under the previous heading. In some of the settings in which we have worked, such group meetings to discuss and plan colleagues' work have been a regular part of the weekly schedule. In a group forum, there is obviously the advantage of benefiting from a wider range of views.

Discussion of 'options'

What we describe as an 'options' discussion is a useful means of planning for new or unknown situations. Workers are often required to go out on new referrals or into new situations with very little information beforehand. The most common situations are where allegations are made of some kind of abuse of children or a referral is received requesting a worker to be involved in a mental health section. These situations can develop very quickly, and it may not be possible to gather background information before a visit is made. In these situations, we have found it very helpful, before making a visit, to sit down with a supervisor/line manager or a colleague and go through the possible strategies that might be used to deal with the range of possible scenarios the worker may find when they make the visit. In a child abuse investigation, for example, it is possible to discuss what might happen if the child is in the house on their own, if the parent will not let the worker enter the house, or if the child is obviously at risk. This means that in the heat of the moment, the worker has a number of planned options to fall back on and so is less likely to be drawn unhelpfully into the family's interactional processes.

Pre- and post-work planning with colleagues

This method is useful in helping a worker analyse their involvement with a service user and in monitoring the effectiveness of their work. Before carrying out the piece of work – for example, making a visit, undertaking a task with a resident, or attending a meeting – the worker discusses with a colleague what they wish to achieve and how they are going to carry it out. Then, having completed the work, the worker again discusses what happened with their colleague, and together they are able to examine the interactional process. The advantage of this method is that the worker is able to get feedback on their performance very soon after the event, often the same day. In some ways, this is similar to the process of supervision, but the main difference is that the worker receives immediate feedback. With formal supervision, it may be two weeks, a month or even longer before the worker sees their supervisor again. Much of the important information will have been forgotten, and the opportunity for learning and improved practice is lost.

One considerable disadvantage of the methods described above is that they are all based on one-sided reports of what has taken place. Only the worker's point of view is available: the service user's view is not heard. The methods that are described below overcome this problem by having the consultant present as the interaction between the worker and the service user is either taking place or being simulated.

Roleplay/sculpting

These are useful methods to use when the option of being present in person is not available. They have a different quality to the methods outlined so far, in that they do not rely on verbal reports and instead can allow an outside consultant access to a visual image of the interaction, as well as some sense of their emotional content. The detail of these techniques is well described in a number of texts (Walrond-Skinner, 1976; Barker, 1981; Burnham, 1986), but their value lies in the fact that by having colleagues 'act out' a particular family or group, it is often possible to identify the interactional process that has taken place between the worker and the service users, and, more particularly, the blocks that are interfering in this process.

Live consultation

Models of live consultation have mainly been developed as methods of practice in the field of family therapy over the last forty years, and as Liddle et al. (1988) have pointed out, the logic of live consultation was built into the theoretical framework underlying the approach:

> Family therapy broke traditional rules about the individual patient's confidentiality by inviting family members to participate in therapy. Once defined as a public event, it was an easy step for family therapy to be observed by others, initially for research and later for team approaches to therapy and supervision. This public nature helped create the most popular forms of family therapy supervision, live and video tape. Family therapy's emphasis on the interactive process also required a method of supervision capable of accessing this process. Therapist recall, process notes, and even audiotapes could not capture the richness and complexity of a family therapy session; consequently, means of direct observation evolved, culminating . . . in the methods of live and videotape supervision. (Liddle et al., 1988, p. 151)

As Liddle et al. identify, the shift from private interaction to public event was a crucial one, for it changed the whole context in which therapy took place. Freud and psychoanalysis had closed the window on therapeutic practice: family therapy opened it up again.

As well as this theoretical shift involved in allowing practice to be observed, there are also many practical advantages for workers. First, having a colleague present is a great support for workers accustomed to working on their own, particularly in situations that are difficult and stressful. It allows a sharing of responsibility and the opportunity to discuss assessments of risk. It also means that the worker who is working directly with the service users can get instant feedback on what is happening from the observing colleague. They can then take the opportunity to make immediate interventions. In our experience, using a model of live consultation is also more effective in terms of time and resources; since much more information can be gathered in one interview or meeting and with the support of a colleague, it is easier to make definite decisions. We have also found that service users generally value the commitment of having two workers involved in their situation.

However, the essential requirement for using live consultation successfully is to continue to maintain a systemic perspective throughout the process. This means that the two workers need to maintain different positions in relation to the service users. Both workers should not work directly with the users: one should maintain a position as an observer while the other is involved with the service user. This is the position illustrated in Figure 3.1.

There are a variety of ways of maintaining these different positions between the two workers and of organising models of live consultation. These are outlined below around two main considerations:

1   the means used to enable the consultant to observe the worker;
2   the means used to enable the consultant and the worker to communicate.

Means of observation

There are a variety of ways in which the consultant can observe the worker while they are at work:

- observing from a position in the same room as the worker and service users;
- observing from an adjoining room via a one-way screen;
- observing from another room via a video camera and monitor.

Means of communication

Similarly, there are a number of ways in which the consultant can communicate with the worker during the course of a session:

- if in the same room as the worker, either by speaking to the worker directly in the service users' hearing or asking the worker to take a break and going out of the room together;
- by the worker leaving the session at times pre-specified or decided by them;
- if outside the room, by knocking on the door as a signal for the worker to leave the session for discussion;
- if outside the room, by entering the room and speaking directly to the worker in the service user's hearing;
- via a telephone link;
- via a microphone linked to a earphone in the worker's ear.

All workers should obtain the service users' informed consent to the use of any of the above methods of observation and communication (Evans, 1987a).

A recent development of the live consultation model is what is known as the 'reflecting team' (Andersen, 1987, 1990). With this approach, the team do not remain invisible behind the one-way screen, but at different points in the session they swap places with the family and the therapist. The family are then able to observe the team members offering 'reflections' about what they have seen.

Use of video/audio facilities

When it is not possible to use a model of live consultation in joint work, another means of achieving direct access to the interactional process between the worker and the service user is to use some means of recording the meeting. The use of video equipment has become fairly common in recent years, particularly for recording interviews with children in cases of sexual abuse, and many agencies have equipment available to make video recordings of interviews. Such recordings offer valuable information, both to the worker and any colleague viewing the tape, and are an excellent means of providing consultation. The technology of audio tape is obviously simpler and cheaper than video, and although it is limited in that it only provides information on the verbal interaction, it still gives a sense of the 'feel' of the interaction. It also has the advantage of being more easily acceptable and less intrusive in the homes of service users and other settings outside offices and clinics (Evans, 1991).

'Time out'/self-consultation

This final method is somewhat paradoxical, in that it is used when the worker is operating on their own without anyone acting as a consultant. However, both authors have found that a simple technique, such as taking a short break in the middle of a contact with service users, is helpful in re-orientating one's thinking, especially if a lot of new information is being presented, or sometimes where very powerful feelings are being expressed. The simple fact of taking a break can also be helpful in giving the service users time to relax and avoid escalating a situation that might be emotionally charged. All that needs to be done is to say to the service users that you wish to take a short break to think about what they have said, or alternatively, to suggest a break, say, to make a cup of tea. The advantage of such breaks is that they give the worker a chance to reflect on the interactional process that has taken place and perhaps determine an alternative way forward. Carr (1986) suggests a number of more detailed methods a solo worker can use to assist their thinking in their work. As with live consultation, these methods should all be agreed with service users in advance.

In this chapter, we have attempted to identify some of the key principles involved in utilising a systemic approach and what the implications are for practice. All of the models suggested are based on the consistent use of an interactional perspective, whether this relates to the relationship with the service users or with colleagues. Although we have talked about each principle separately, in many work situations, workers will be thinking about and using a number of these principles simultaneously.

4 The central triangular context

Social care work often takes place in very complex contexts. We propose one central context as a focus for this work, which can help cut through much of the complexity without oversimplifying, as well as being of value in relatively simpler situations. It is the triangular relationship between the *worker*, the *agency* for whom they work, and the *service user* who receives a service from the agency (see Figure 4.1).

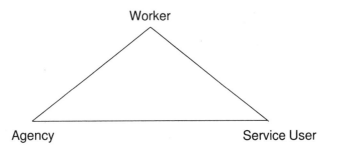

Figure 4.1   The central triangular context

The worker

We use this term to emphasise a particular 'work' function of seeking to help someone else with the social need they are experiencing (see Chapter 1). Work contracts limit the benefits for the worker to money and holidays and serve as a check on workers who transgress work boundaries, as recent scandals in residential settings have indicated. None the less, workers bring to their work relevant experiences and personal attributes from outside their work and will need to monitor the helpfulness or otherwise of these.

The agency

This term denotes the organisational base from which the worker encounters service users and which legitimises their activities. The worker's identity card, required by most agencies, is a potent symbol of that legitimacy. The agency is thus more than one person: it invariably includes managers and workers, and at times councillors (social services departments) and service users (some voluntary organisations). As well as people, the agency comprises institutional processes such as policies, procedures, rules and a working ethos. Agencies as organisations can be analysed in a number of different ways (Perrow, 1970; Handy, 1985; Morgan, 1986; Hasenfeld, 1992a). Morgan (1986) elaborates the interesting thesis that organisational analysis is a process of using different metaphors which specify certain attributes or processes within organisations. His metaphors include a machine, an organism, a brain, a prison, a system of government and an instrument of domination. He suggests that our attitude to organisations should not be constrained by any one of these metaphors.

The agency also has a physical dimension, namely the different settings from which it undertakes its work: a purpose-built day care centre, a drop-in centre, a fieldwork office. The geographical location of the setting and other internal aspects, such as accessibility for disabled people and open-plan offices, will have a major influence on how social care is delivered.

The agency's approach to a given need will be determined partly externally, particularly by those who fund its activities, and partly internally. In the more bureaucratic agencies, upper managers and councillors develop policies which can influence specific practices. Some such agencies allow influence upward through the hierarchy, whereby workers can influence policy through working groups and more informal contacts.

The service user

This third major participant in the process of meeting social need is undoubtedly the most difficult to name. This difficulty arises predominantly from the conflicting ideologies which constitute the context for the personal social services in this period of transition towards increased privatisation of welfare and increased power for service users (Clarke, 1993). Five terms seem to be in use: 'consumer', 'customer', 'client', 'service user', 'user'. It is perhaps a comment on the constant flux of this transition and the reluctance of many people within the personal social services to accept the progression towards privatisation that no clear consensus about terminology has emerged.

'Consumer' and 'customer' are terms which stem from a growing awareness of people's rights to receive appropriate services, which continues to be fuelled by John Major's predilection for charters. However, both terms are redolent of the dominant materialism of the past Thatcherite decade and are thus incompatible with other values inherent in public social services. For this reason, we reject them.

'Client' is embedded in the language of professionalism. As such, it supports an unequal distribution of power between the professional and the layperson, an inequality which is inappropriate to a genuine participation in service delivery. The decreasing use of this term seems to have occurred partly as those who seek professional power and autonomy have begun to lose their grip within the personal social services and partly as a result of the Thatcherite assault on interest groups such as professions. Largely because of this inherent inequality of power, we support its demise.

'User' has a number of weaknesses. It seems to suggest a somewhat functional and potentially dehumanising relationship. It is damaging to human relationships when people 'use' people as if they are objects. Moreover, 'user' in contexts such as drug and alcohol dependency carries the connotation of abusing or misusing.

The term 'user' also tends to emphasise a distinction between those who use services and those who provide them. This seems to run counter to recent attempts to encourage people to participate in the planning and delivery of services and not merely see themselves as passive recipients – much as the medical term 'patient' does.

In community care contexts, 'user' is often juxtaposed with 'carer'. However, these words define only one aspect of the relationship between people experiencing social need. A 'user' may be a 'carer's' mother, and this latter aspect of the relationship may predominate and be a principal factor inhibiting the adjustment of both people to the 'user's' increasing dependency on their adult offspring (Evans, 1985). Moreover, the terms obscure the fact that once those who care for others receive services from personal social service agencies, they equally become 'users'. King (1993) indicates an even more starkly inappropriate facet of the 'user'/'carer' dichotomy when so-called 'carers' abuse their relatives.

We find 'service user' the most acceptable of current terms, although it can at times be cumbersome. Its strength lies in its relative neutrality and the fact that it accepts the influence that legislation and government thinking have on activities within the personal social services. It also emphasises appropriately the primary relationship which individual recipients of services have with the agency that delivers them, thus counterbalancing an earlier and often misleading overemphasis on their relationship with the worker. It is not possible to speak of 'workers and *their* service users' as it was 'workers and *their* clients'.

Another advantage of this term is that it places one person – the person with learning disabilities, mental health difficulties, physical or sensory impairment – in a more direct relationship with the agency. This person has been known at different times as the '*referred* client' or in medical settings as the '*index* patient' and is identified at the start of any work. Even in community work, which appears to eschew such a term, a group of people experiencing a common social need is often identified initially, whether by the funding body or key community members. Those people who are identified at the outset in all work settings are often particularly powerless: children, black women, demented older people, working-class tenants. Their experiences of social need are constantly in danger of being submerged under the experiences of their more powerful relatives, neighbours and workers. It is advisable that their experience should be constantly in the thoughts of workers and their agencies.

This triangular relationship thus involves two people and one organisational base. The reason we have placed the worker at the top of the triangle in Figure 1.1 is not because they necessarily have any greater value or power in the interaction – it is our experience that most workers reflect about these three in descending order: service user, agency, worker; therefore, we are simply seeking to redress this focus.

Some examples of this relationship would include: a home care assistant working for a private organisation visiting an elderly, physically handicapped couple; a community worker funded by the health authority to improve the welfare of residents on a housing estate; a local authority day care worker running a group for people who are depressed and isolated.

In most situations, it is easy for us to recognise the triangle whenever we are engaged in working in social care. However, as the boundaries between agencies become more diffused in inter-agency work and workers construct their own employment packages with different agencies, it is occasionally necessary to be clear about the organisational base for a given piece of work. More typically, it is easy for workers to underestimate the influence of their organisational base in the work they seek to do, and for both workers and agencies to lose sight of the initial, referred service user(s) when the work has progressed for some time. If you have become stuck in your work or are about to embark upon a new piece of work, a useful question is always:

> *What constitutes the triangular context for this particular work with social need?*

Why this particular triangle?

This question is perhaps logically preceded by another: 'Why focus on a three-way relationship at all as a central interactional context?' The answer is that a triangle is the simplest context which none the less introduces some complexity.

In many disciplines, an important distinction is made between two and more than two, but a less important distinction between three, four, five, six, and so on. In geometry, for example, two points are joined by a one-dimensional *line*, whereas once three or more points are joined, a two-dimensional *area* is formed. Several languages, including Anglo-Saxon, distinguish grammatically between one, two and more than two, and semantically between 'two' and 'many'. In human relationships, too, triangles have a reputation of being difficult, but largely in contrast with the relative simplicity of two-person relationships. Biggs (1994) makes a similar point, although he is discussing the different triangle of service user, carer and worker in community care settings.

This particular triangular relationship has impressed us over the years as the 'minimum sufficient context' for explaining and determining how people work with social needs. In addition to its simplicity, its strength is threefold, in that it includes:

1   the referred person, thus potentially empowering an individual with a particular need;
2   the human relationship between two people, which can play a key part in resolving social need;
3   the organisational base, which sets the whole endeavour in a social context beyond an interpersonal encounter.

Its central significance is endorsed by Taylor and Devine (1993).

The literature of social work, from Biestek (1957) to Payne (1991), has consistently stressed the importance of the relationship between the worker and the service user. We would wish to endorse that view, recognising the extent to which many service users appear to value this relationship (Mayer and Timms, 1970; Sainsbury et al., 1982; Rees and Wallace, 1982; Fisher, 1983; Cheetham et al., 1992). We also suspect that high on the list of factors influencing people to work in social care is their genuine interest in or enjoyment of relationships with service users.

However, the context of working in social care is not merely interpersonal, it is also social and institutional, as Payne (1991) emphasises. Social work, he claims, is a 'socially constructed activity' (Payne, 1991, p. 7). While not disputing this, we would argue that wider social influences impinge less

immediately and directly on most workers' practice than does the organisational base for that practice. Only the agency can sack workers, thus preventing them from working in social care, although wider social influences may
inhibit or restrict that work.

In effect, the agency is a mediator of wider societal policies, values, powers
and resources (Hugman, 1991). The state organises its response to social need
through agencies, and through agencies mandates individual workers to
tackle that need. The agency is thus the predominant context within which
worker and service user engage in work.

There are, clearly, ever-widening contexts which surround the three participants of this triangular relationship, and which eventually surround the
triangle as a whole. Kingston (1979) outlines several which surround the
worker and the service user. The NHS and Community Care Act (1990)
necessitates that agencies will operate more interdependently within the network of welfare agencies: statutory, voluntary and private. None the less, we
think there is value in starting with this triangle as the hub of all work with
social need.

As can be seen from Figure 4.2, a triangular relationship comprises six sets
of relationships: not only the three two-way relationships (solid line) of
worker and service user, service user and agency, agency and worker, but
also the three three-way relationships (dotted line) of worker with agency
and service user, service user with agency, and worker and agency with
worker and service user.

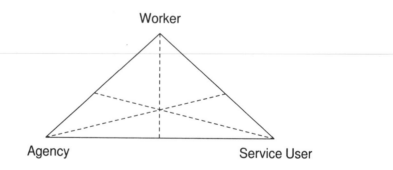

Figure 4.2   Three-way relationships in the triangular process

A triangular relationship also comprises three individual points. A systemic approach is concerned with individuals, but only with those attributes,
attitudes and behaviours which are relevant to their context. For instance,
aspects of the worker which are particularly relevant to the context of working in social care have largely been reported elsewhere: practice method
(Howe, 1987; Coulshed, 1991), practice style (Heron, 1975), values (Howe,

1987; Shardlow, 1989; CCETSW, 1989a, 1995), personal experience (Rees and Wallace, 1982), emotional readiness (Kadushin, 1976; Atherton, 1986), intellectual readiness (CCETSW, 1989a, 1995) intuition (Jordan, 1979; England, 1986). Within the limits of this book, therefore, we shall concentrate only on the relationships *within* the triangle, and not on the individual points.

Two-way relationships within the triangle

Worker, service user and agency come together in three simple, dyadic relationships: worker–service user; worker–agency; service user–agency. These three relationships differ in many respects, which we will explore below. However, common to them all are two central dimensions: partnership and power. The role of power within partnership is of particular interest.

Partnership

'Partnership' has been a buzzword of the late 1980s and the early 1990s. Its appeal rests in its focus on values such as collectivity, co-operation and equality, as opposed to those of individualism, competition and inequality. Partnerships have been increasingly sought and formed at an international level, notably between East and West. Within the UK personal social services, they have been forged between statutory and independent sectors; between different statutory sectors, such as health, housing and social services; between educational and practice organisations, and between workers and service users. However, like '*liberté, egalité, fraternité*' and other slogans of the past, 'partnership' is a dangerously imprecise term which can sweep people along unthinkingly. Howe (1992) goes further, describing it as 'promiscuous'.

One principal danger rests in the way in which 'partnership', by concentrating on communalities, obscures the reality of differences in aims and, particularly, power between partners. These differences can be perceived behind many current partnerships between service users on the one hand and workers and agencies on the other. For example, the requirement under the Access to Personal Files Act (1987) that service users should have access to their agency records has stimulated the growth of 'shared recording'. In her study of shared recording in East Sussex Social Services Department, Raymond (1989) reports how this experience was generally valued by service users. However, she cites occasions where the reality of power differentials mars the experience of partnership for service users:

> You feel a bit pressurised. You've got to knuckle under and if it comes to it, just bite your tongue. (Raymond, 1989, p. 13)

On other occasions, service users even lack the power of knowledge about such recording:

> I wasn't told anything about looking at the case records. I was told it was private – to them only. (Thoburn, 1992, p. 73)

There has been a similar impetus towards a growing use of contracts (Cordern and Preston-Shoot, 1987a) which can empower service users to participate more fully in the various processes entailed in working with social need. However, in the agreements enshrined in such contracts, service users do not always give 'real consent' which stems from genuine choice. Consent can be extracted under threat, for example, of the Child Protection Order (Thomas and Forbes, 1989), or it can be assumed to have been given, for example, by more severely demented service users, in what Fisher (1990) calls 'passive consent'.

Moreover, the binding force of a contract rests, in the last analysis, on sanctions. With power largely in the hands of the worker and the agency, they can apply sanctions for breaches of contract on the part of service users by taking statutory powers (Platt, 1993) or withholding resources. Users' sanctions are often limited to legal redress and complaints systems. Even though the NHS and Community Care Act (1990) has supported the development of complaints systems, their effectiveness as a service users' sanction awaits full demonstration.

Clearly, partnerships are likely to work best when differences in power are overt rather than covert. The Family Rights Group (1991) recognises that common aims and shared information are realistically achievable features of partnerships between families and state agencies, but not equal power. Government also recognises power differentials between service users and agencies in implementing both Community Care (DoH and Scottish Office, 1991a, p. 14) and the Children Act (DoH, 1991).

However, such recognition does not obviate the need to seek to minimise power differences. Holman (1992) criticises the Children Act (1989) for not achieving a better balance of power between local authorities and parents, for example, through family advocacy units and through collective and not just individual processes enabling parents and children to participate. It is interesting to contrast the British *Children Act* (1989) with the New Zealand *Children, Young Persons and their Families Act* (1989), which places most of the decisionmaking power in the hands of wider family units, and not with agencies.

Genuine participation in partnerships is only possible with some redistribution of power. Arnstein (1971) outlines a progressive scheme, whereby individual citizens can exercise increasing participatory power (Figure 4.3). Howe (1992) also develops a four-position matrix in which genuine partnership arises from participation plus choice.

Citizen control Delegated power Partnership	Degrees of citizen power
Placation Consultation Informing	Degrees of tokenism
Therapy Manipulation	Non-participation

Figure 4.3   Degrees of citizen participation

Genuine partnerships are more likely to be achieved if they include some of the following processes:

- identifying and stating common aims and values;
- listing the partners involved;
- recognising relevant differences in aims and values;
- recognising differences in resources and other powers between the partners;
- allocating tasks and functions according to the different abilities of partners;
- delineating and allocating a lead role, when necessary;
- ensuring an essential, minimal flow of information between partners;
- identifying and establishing mechanisms for resolving differences.

Several of these processes are outlined, for example, for multi-disciplinary work in child protection (DHSS and Welsh Office, 1988).

Worker–service user

The importance of this relationship is emphasised throughout the literature, not only by social work professionals (England, 1986; Howe, 1987; Payne,

1991) but also others (Hasenfeld, 1992a) and in the accounts of service users (Fisher, 1983; Rees and Wallace, 1982). Hasenfeld (1992a) suggests that this relationship is particularly important under four circumstances, when:

1   clients must have continuous contact with the agency;
2   the work requires extensive penetration into the service user's biographical time and space;
3   interpersonal relationships are actually a major mode of intervention;
4   the stakes of the intervention are high.

It is possible to see this relationship in four main ways:

● a human relationship;
● a power relationship;
● a working relationship;
● a helping relationship.

The human relationship

The emphatic message from consumer studies is that service users primarily seek basic human processes in their encounters with workers. In their review of consumer studies at that time, Rees and Wallace (1982) cluster many of these processes under three main headings: that workers show personal interest and concern in service users' well-being; that workers adopt the informal and sympathetic approach towards service users typified by a 'good friend'; that workers are able to put service users at ease, particularly through an accepting and non-judgmental attitude. Other basic human qualities welcomed by service users include honesty, openness and trust (Mayer and Timms, 1970; Thoburn, 1980).

Despite these clear messages from service users and some professionals, human qualities such as these do not receive universal acclaim throughout the professional literature. Some workers seek to enhance their effectiveness by training in methods which promote antithetical qualities and methods such as neutrality and paradoxical statements (Palazzoli et al., 1980). Moreover, in their comprehensive summaries of the requirements of qualifying social workers, CCETSW (1989a, 1995) totally overlook such qualities in their emphasis on the skills, values and knowledge which can be acquired or improved through training.

The power relationship

Power is at the heart of the relationship between worker and service user. In the UK, workers are mostly white, while disproportionate numbers of service users are black. What black workers there are, Hugman (1991) suggests, are mostly located in low-prestige areas of work, such as residential care. Moreover, the majority of service users are from the working classes, while most workers, if not middle-class themselves, will undoubtedly represent the interests of the dominant classes, as mediated by their agency (Hugman, 1991). Workers, certainly those in paid employment, are likely to be aged between 16 and 65, while increasing numbers of service users are outside that age bracket.

Most service users and workers are alike in being women (Davis and Brook, 1985). Although gender is thus not typically a source of power differentials, it will clearly be so in some encounters. Moreover, when women come together to work on a social need, they share a common experience of a patriarchal society, which can enrich and strengthen their work (Hanmer and Statham, 1988). These basic institutional sources of power differentials through race, class, age and gender are often compounded in multiple disadvantage.

Hasenfeld (1992b) identifies four other sources of power which workers can have in their relationships with service users:

- 'the power of expertise', derived from their access to specialised knowledge;
- 'referent power', or the power to persuade, which stems from their interpersonal skills;
- 'legitimate power', through appealing to dominant cultural values and authoritative norms;
- 'gatekeeping power', as members of organisations which control critical resources.

Two additional sources of power are:

- 'positional power', as an accepted and integral member of the state welfare network, with a capacity, for example, to cut through the red tape; this power can be much appreciated by service users (Phillimore, 1981);
- 'coercive or statutory power', whereby workers can use legal statutes to insist that their wishes are followed.

While 'expertise', 'referent power' and 'legitimate power' accrue to the worker as an individual, their 'gatekeeping', 'positional' and 'coercive' power are all derived from their membership of an agency.

It is important that workers are aware of these powers and seek to maximise their advantages and minimise their disadvantages. Dale et al. (1986), in their descriptions of 'dangerous professionals', illustrate well the risk inherent in being ambivalent about the use of power.

'Service users', in their turn, often lose power in the very process of becoming a service user, by being 'socially constructed as objects of an occupation' (Hugman, 1991, p. 43). Certainly, the stigma experienced by many service users may diminish their self-esteem and influence, and workers may also perceive and treat people as in some sense 'diminished' simply because they are service users.

The concept of 'service user' or 'client' is contrasted with that of 'citizen' by Jordan (1987), Croft and Beresford (1989) and Biehal (1993). A citizen is not only a potential service user but also involved, through democratic processes, in controlling those services. When a service user 'threatens', as it may be perceived by a worker, to consult their councillor, member of parliament or local authority ombudsperson or to evoke legal processes over dissatisfaction with a given worker or agency, they are doing no more than evoking this other facet of their power relationship with the worker.

Equality of power should not automatically be seen as the preferred condition within the worker–service user relationship. Rees and Wallace (1982) distinguish between two sets of consumer opinion. Some service users – usually those who are well-educated, economically secure and confident with officialdom – wish to share power and decisionmaking with workers. However, others – often poor, with a tendency to be submissive when confronted with officials – prefer the worker to exhibit their expertise and exercise authority over them. Clearly, in a complementary relationship, workers can exercise their greater power beneficially on behalf of less powerful service users, and with their approval. The question is: do they?

None the less, there will be many occasions when workers and service users seek to minimise the power differential between them. When the differential is an institutional one of race, gender, class or age, the worker's first priority is to increase their own awareness of their potential to discriminate (Dominelli, 1988), and to counteract it actively.

When the differential arises from the worker's greater powers outlined above, there are four major strategies which the worker can adopt to increase the service user's power.

First, the worker can seek to inform the service user fully: of choices available to them in terms of resources, legal and other support, and of that knowledge which constitutes the worker's expertise.

Second, the worker can encourage the service user's full participation in the various processes of working with social need, including decisionmaking (Bamford, 1990). Service users are critical when they have not been consulted, even if they are aware that it is the authority which will make the decisions (Thoburn, 1992). Both of these strategies are endorsed by studies of service users who are at the receiving end of statutory child care and protection (Thoburn, 1980).

A third strategy is to encourage the service user to enlist the help of others who will support their case. This can be done informally through inviting friends, neighbours or relatives to key meetings, including conferences, reviews and planning meetings. Some workers may inappropriately seek to dissuade users from having such people present at meetings, from such laudable motives as confidentiality. Other workers may not be aware exactly whom service users wish to invite: some ethnic minority service users would prefer a person in authority, such as a GP, to family members (Virdee, 1992). Formal advocacy is also available to service users, not only for children through the guardians ad litem system, but increasingly for people who are unable to state their position clearly, through dementia and other mental health problems or learning disabilities (Fennell et al., 1988). For example, self-advocacy groups for people with learning disabilities (Simons, 1993) can achieve empowerment through collective action.

A fourth strategy is to listen ever harder to how service users define the need they experience, and other aspects of their lives, including their encounters with workers and agencies. It is mainly for this reason that we have included findings from consumer studies in this section, so that the voices of service users can be heard attempting to define their relationship with workers.

It is an interesting disjunction that while service users seem predominantly concerned with workers' attributes (the person) and their work effectiveness (the outcome), most professional workers seem mainly concerned with competencies, be they skills or knowledge (the processes). The word 'professional' is used advisedly here, since we suspect that the key to this disjunction lies in workers and others seeking to increase their power by concentrating on those characteristics which differentiate them as professionals from lay people – namely, those skills, knowledge and values which are achieved through training and are part of professional acculturalisation, what Rojek et al. (1988) call 'received ideas'.

While it can be argued that service users are less likely to be aware of the skills through which workers can show parts of themselves and achieve effective outcomes, we would maintain that it behoves workers to attend more to service users' definitions of the relationship they wish with workers and their agencies. However, we believe, as does Fisher (1983), that service users' opinions should have a strong influence but should not be the sole determinant.

This injunction to heed the service users' own statements about their position holds as much at the micro-level of personal interaction as at the macro-level of consumer studies research. It is important that workers learn to suspend the processes which lead them to impose their own meanings prematurely ('Oh, it's another part III referral!') on to service users' subjective statements about their own lives (Rojek et al., 1988).

There are also other processes which can help redress the power imbalance between workers and service users. Beresford (1994) and Harrison and Beresford (1994) report on the developing trend towards involving service users in the process of training student social workers, including assessing them. Evans (1991) elaborates further how service users can be involved in this assessment process. Not only can specific service users gain some power over their student workers by contributing to their assessment, but also, in a more general way, service users can begin to loosen the stranglehold of professional self-regulation which is currently kept on entry into social work. Similar processes are entirely appropriate and already in use in social care.

The working relationship

The relationship we are concerned to describe in this book is essentially a working one. One important corollary of this is that the worker should indeed be seen to 'work'. Rees and Wallace (1982) describe how service users generally appreciate active workers who 'do things' for them – for example, by giving advice or making practical arrangements. This practical action is often interpreted (we consider, quite rightly) as a sign of concern and is generally more easily demonstrated by social care workers than social workers.

Another important aspect of 'working' is that the relationship is, in itself, a means and not an end. The work has a goal of effectively reducing or meeting a social need. Service users also make this distinction: they generally express considerable satisfaction in their human relationships with workers, but much less satisfaction in the outcome or effectiveness of the work undertaken (Rees, 1978; Sainsbury et al., 1982). This relative dissatisfaction places an onus on workers and agencies to emphasise the evaluation of effectiveness in the work, which we shall address in Chapter 5.

At times, however, 'work' can become equated with 'busy-ness'. There are still many residential homes for older people in which care assistants have no time to stop and listen to the residents, and many fieldwork teams where it would be considered idleness to be sitting at a desk, thinking or reading a relevant journal. Clearly, much current social care work takes place in contexts of heavy workloads and insufficient staff (Bamford, 1990), when most staff have too much to do. However, effective work requires purposeful action (Howe, 1987), and it is only through thinking that purposes can be divined.

One important facet of working relationships in the caring professions is the regulation of an appropriate emotional distance: one which is not too close and not too distant. A number of influences encourage the service user and worker towards closeness. First and foremost is the importance of recognising, understanding and empathising with the service user's experience of social need, sometimes called a process of 'individuation' (Bamford, 1990; Payne, 1991). Often, the service user's experience of the problem – be it poverty, loss, discrimination, or violence – will be of a highly emotional nature, which can lead to what England (1986) describes as an 'intimate encounter'. Moreover, as described above, service users generally indicate that they are more satisfied with a warm, trusting relationship with a 'good friend' than a detached and distant professional (Rees and Wallace, 1982).

However, there are many influences which promote distance in the working relationship. Workers may seek to distance themselves from service users for a number of reasons. Service users can become overburdened by pessimism concerning their plight, overwhelmed by the emotions evoked by their experience or constrained by a particular view of their need. At such times, it is unhelpful for the worker to become too identified with the service user, for fear of becoming similarly unable to meet the need.

Workers who are confronted regularly with highly distressing human suffering can also find it necessary to distance themselves somewhat from that suffering in order to reduce their own distress and prevent burn-out. We have found that inexperienced student social workers will often identify themselves particularly closely with service users' distress, not having learned the painful necessity of distancing themselves somewhat.

Hugman (1991) suggests that a further reason for workers distancing themselves from service users is to retain a degree of control over the encounter. In a sense, workers require a level of control over the emotions which could potentially inhibit their work. Distance can be seen as a mechanism of control. An appropriate emotional distance will need to be achieved in each work–service user relationship. This may be more difficult in certain working contexts: for example, in group care settings when staff and service users share intimate physical tasks or in field and clinical work when areas of work such as sexual relationships can potentially increase intimacy. It may also be more difficult to achieve to the mutual satisfaction of worker and service user when their emotional needs clash.

The helping relationship

Much social care work is premised on the tacitly agreed and complementary relationship between 'helper' and 'helped' (Jordan, 1979; Egan, 1982). However, it is not only in social control or statutory work that this complementarity does not necessarily apply. Rees (1978) describes how many working-class service users feel a strong sense of shame in seeking help over social need. Furthermore, many service users express reservations about the helpfulness of their workers if they are not of the same gender and age and have not themselves experienced a similar need (Rees and Wallace, 1982).

One approach to these two difficulties is the development of self-help. Adams (1990) suggests further advantages in self-help: that it involves self-management, empowerment, is anti-bureaucratic and promotes co-operation. Moreover, he indicates three different types of self-help, which are in effect defined by the different relationships between the worker, their agency and the service user (see Chapter 5).

Questions to ask about your relationship with a current service user:

> *Am I behaving towards the service user in an appropriately concerned, friendly, accepting manner?*
> *What sources of power am I drawing on in this relationship? Am I failing to encourage the service user to draw on theirs?*
> *Is the degree of closeness in this relationship appropriate to the work?*
> *How much is this a mutually agreed helping relationship?*
> *Should I ask the service user for their views on any of the above questions?*

Worker–agency

Although the relationship between the worker and the service user occupies a central position in the literature, the worker's relationship with the agency for which they work can become a central preoccupation. Occupational stress can be the result of the worker's treatment by their agency as much as distress caused by service users. In his elaboration of the metaphor of the organisation as an 'instrument of domination', Morgan (1986) concentrates on the effects of the physical conditions of the work setting on the workforce through illness and death. While these effects also occur in the personal social services, it is the social and emotional effects of the organisational base which are most pronounced. Of these, Morgan (1986) describes workaholism but neglects other important factors such as burn-out and lack of autonomy.

There are times when the adverse effects of work appear to be caused solely by individual service users. Female social workers are more likely to be murdered by male service users (Rojek et al., 1988). More recent studies of assaults on workers (Leadbetter, 1993) suggest that a high proportion occur in residential and day care settings, and that men are now more likely to be assaulted than women. However, the responsibility for even such occurrences as these can also be laid, to a degree, at the door of agencies whose managers have not seen assault as a priority and have not taken sufficient steps to ensure the safety of their workers (Littlechild, 1993).

The relationship between workers and agencies is a complex and crucial one, which is demanding increasing attention, for example, in the competences required of qualified social workers (CCETSW, 1989a, 1995). We will focus on three aspects of that relationship:

1   the congruence between the aims and values of worker and agency;

2   the power imbalance between the two;
3   the extent to which one maximises or minimises the potential
    effectiveness of the other.

Congruence

Much of the dissatisfaction workers experience with their agencies stems from a lack of congruence between their respective aims and values. This is particularly the case for workers in statutory agencies. Their principal motivation is often to help people in distress or suffering from disadvantage. However, they are increasingly finding that agencies such as social services and social work departments demand that they concentrate on restricting the allocation of scarce resources and imposing constraints on unwilling clients, and that probation services adhere to justice rather than welfare models. Even voluntary agencies are increasingly contracted by social services departments to help them fulfil their statutory duties.

It is no easy matter for many workers to discover the aims and values of their agency, let alone assess their compatibility with their own. It seems that the larger the organisation, the greater the plurality of values and the less the accessibility to statements of aims. Small voluntary or private organisations often make clear statements of aims and objectives as part of their public presentation. Likewise, small units within larger organisations, such as residential units or family centres, may seek to clarify their aims for referrers and service users alike. Moreover, with a small workforce and an even smaller number of managers, there is relatively little difficulty in achieving agreement about such aims.

Social services departments, social work departments and probation services, on the other hand, have tended not to make such clear statements. As Bamford (1989) claims, their values are often transmitted through an unarticulated socialisation process. This is partly because their aims are largely determined externally by social policy, and partly because many individuals within the organisation might claim the right to determine aims, be they councillors or officers. Some upper managers, collectively or individually, draw up statements of purpose or mission statements (Coulshed, 1990). However, these are often not communicated directly to workers, but reside in the minutes of upper management meetings or council papers. Most recently, in a climate of charterism, social services departments have been making clear statements of intent to the public they serve. However, it remains to be seen how much such public statements inform the internal processes which influence workers.

One strategy for workers to adopt, having identified potential differences in aims between themselves and their agency, is to seek to match them more carefully. One of the authors applied this approach in a social services fieldwork setting as a means of achieving his aim of being able to work with families using a systemic approach. Recognising that the office needed to provide a range of services to the local community and that the number of staff available to do this was limited, he decided that instead of *asking* his manager for something (a reduced caseload in order to undertake specialised work with families), he *offered* him something that was useful to him as a manager: he agreed to make an assessment, and do any follow-up work necessary, of any case the manager wished to give him. No doubt, many workers would regard this approach as extremely foolish, but that is to ignore the context of a social services department and the constraints which govern a manager's position. The last thing a manager needs in a community-based team are workers who want to operate an elitest model of work with a select group of service users: this does not meet the obligation of the manager to provide a service to the whole community.

In this particular example, the effect of the author offering to take any case the manager allocated was not that he was exploited, but rather that the manager regarded him as a positive resource and, in fact, became quite selective about the cases he wished him to look at. The manager also became very interested and supportive of the family work the author was doing.

Power imbalance

In the event of an excessive conflict of aims and values between agency managers and workers, there is little doubt who stands to lose most. Managers have the power to hire and fire and, through references, to influence future hirings: what Elliott (1980) calls 'power over' the workforce. Weber's typology of domination (Mouzelis, 1979) indicates how other sources of power can accrue to managers, including traditional practices and charisma.

The growth of managerialism in a climate of heightened public accountability for service delivery and for cost-effectiveness (Bamford, 1990; Hugman, 1991) has increased this imbalance of power. As Bamford claims:

> The growth in managerial power . . . threatens to subjugate ordinary morality to organisational morality. (Bamford, 1989, p. 154)

Moreover, these functional power differentials between managers and workers are frequently reinforced by institutional discrimination, whereby managers will tend to be male and white, while a greater proportion of workers will be female and black (Hugman, 1991; Davis and Brook, 1985; Hasenfeld, 1992a). There is, moreover, some evidence that the proportion of black managers is now decreasing (Peters, 1993). It is likely, too, that a disproportionate number of upper managers in the personal social services are able-bodied.

One response to this sense of powerlessness within the agency is for the worker to develop coping mechanisms. Sherman and Wenocur (1983) outline some of these mechanisms, such as capitulation, withdrawal, specialisation and self-victimisation.

Another response is for the worker to attempt to increase their power. First, they can improve their knowledge and understanding of how the agency works as an organisation: its formal and informal structures; its decisionmaking processes; its main policies and procedures; those key people who exercise power beyond their hierarchical position (the equivalent of the celebrated school caretaker).

Second, the worker can ally with fellow workers in creating a collective powerbase from which to push upwards through existing hierarchies and counterbalance the predominant downward pressure. These alliances can be formed within existing organisations that can influence the agency, such as unions or professional associations. They can also be more informal alliances between work colleagues to influence agency policies and practices. One of the authors worked collectively with colleagues in a social services department to develop a workload management scheme which was accepted by middle managers and gave workers increased power to regulate their own workloads. Both authors believe that workers can also increase their control over their practice in the current climate of increasing quality assurance in agencies by being involved in developing with colleagues reliable methods for evaluating the quality of their own practice and then agreeing these with managers.

Third, the worker can adopt a number of different roles which are particularly orientated towards achieving effective work outcomes in an organisational context. Weissman et al. (1983) identify the following roles:

- the diagnostician;
- the expediter;
- the care manager;
- the advocate;
- the service developer
- the organisational reformer.

Maximising potential

Most social services agencies have a considerable potential to work effectively with social need. This potential rests in: the differentiated expertise of the agency's total workforce; the varied functions which it espouses or with which it is endowed by law; the physical resources at its disposal; the agency's position within the social welfare network.

However, the individual worker does not always fulfil that potential when working with a particular service user. Sometimes, this arises simply out of ignorance: a relatively new worker may know neither which day centre will be most suitable for an elderly person nor who can tell them. Sometimes, however, it is likely to stem from unrealistic expectations and blinkered attitudes.

One widely-held expectation among many workers is that their line manager will be able to help them develop the quality of their practice, an expectation shared and endorsed by many line managers. However, it is increasingly becoming an unrealistic expectation, due to two processes: the increasing specialisation of workers, stimulated by recent legislation; the increasing emphasis by agencies on generalised managerial expertise for its managers, rather than specialist practice abilities. To avoid the worker and manager becoming frustrated at unmet practitioner expectations for expertise on practice, it would seem much better that they agree to the worker seeking specialist practice guidance from other workers: for example, in peer/team supervision, or from others in a consultative capacity within and outside the agency (see Chapter 3).

Many workers have preferred ways of approaching social need which can inhibit their ability to draw from the agency's full range of functions. These can include prejudices against work settings such as residential care for children or child and family guidance. They can also include preferences for different types of work: therapy, advocacy, practical resources. Dimmock and Dungworth (1983) sought to persuade workers with a preference for family therapy to look to the full range of powers and resources available in agencies to help families experiencing need.

Agencies, too, can maximise workers' potential, and hence the effectiveness of the agency as a whole. Proper salary structures, physical work conditions, workloads, administrative support, supervision and training form a desirable baseline which is difficult to achieve in many social service agencies in the present economic climate. Beyond this baseline, agencies could, for example, adopt some of the principles advocated by BASW's staff care campaign of the late 1980s and early 1990s, foster meetings for black staff members and women, and develop and implement policies to protect workers from violence (Littlechild, 1993).

Questions to ask yourself are:

Are my agency and I getting the most out of each other? If not, what seem to be the obstacles on my part?

What are the main areas of disagreement between myself and other agency staff about aims or values? Is there any solution?

Which other workers or managers in the agency can I ally with in order to increase my power over key issues?

Service user–agency

The encounter between service user and agency is for many the starkest experience of the gulf between a vulnerable individual and the unbending edifice of the state. It is not only statutory agencies which mediate the influence and interests of the state (Hugman, 1991); voluntary agencies also do so in their reliance upon state funding, particularly within the current contract culture and the reliance on patronage from influential people. Private agencies are fulfilling a key role in government policies of privatisation. Much of this experience of a gulf stems from the conformist and impersonal workings of bureaucracies which respond to unique and individual distress inadequately and with difficulty. It is further compounded by structural differences whereby agencies tend to represent the interests of white males from the dominant classes, whereas service users are mainly female, working-class and disproportionately black (Hugman, 1991).

The research into service users' opinions indicates that they are generally more dissatisfied with agencies than with their individual workers (Rees and Wallace, 1982). Many service users are found to be quite ignorant of the services offered by agencies; these would include service users for whom English is not their first language or who cannot read English. Often, service users have inappropriate expectations of how agencies can help. Older people have generally been found to have lower expectations than other client groups, which can limit the services they do receive. It is noticeable that the charter movement (DoH, 1994) offers high expectations for consumers of services, without ensuring the consumer power or agency resources to realise those expectations. Generally, appropriate information about services and reasonable expectations can ensure a more satisfactory delivery of services.

Many black clients are dissatisfied with social services departments, seeing them as 'white' organisations, and as such, irrelevant to their needs (Sone, 1993). The explicit requirements in recent legislation – the NHS and Community Care Act (1990), the Children Act (1989) and the Criminal Justice Act (1991) – for anti-discriminatory practices provide a promising springboard to change this dissatisfaction. However, firm policies and detailed practices will be needed to ensure implementation.

One such policy is ethnic monitoring. Francis (1993b) cites a recent survey which suggests that, at that time, well over half the social services departments responding had yet to implement ethnic monitoring. One argument put forward for this low level was an abhorrence of labelling: this clearly indicated a continuing ignorance of the purposes of ethnic monitoring – to ensure that services sensitive to culture and religion can be planned realistically.

For years, service users expected to have little power in their relationships with agencies. Morgan (1986, p. 159) outlines 14 sources of power available to the agency which are not available to the service user. As 'service users', they have had little influence on the provision of resources and delivery of services, although as 'citizens', they have been able to enter into democratic state processes. Beresford and Croft (1981) indicated how infrequently social services at that time involved people outside the agency in planning and delivering services.

However, there are signs that service users are gaining power in their relationships with agencies. Lindsay and Rayner (1993) report an innovative and successful project within the Children's Society in Cleveland in which five young people with experience of being in care helped in the process of selecting new staff. King (1993) reports an initiative in the London Borough of Haringey, wherein mental health service users received training to become consultants to mental health practitioners.

The growth of consumerism and an emphasis on user participation has become a fertile ground for this increase in user power. As Director of Hertfordshire Social Services Department, Herbert Laming (1988), now Chief Inspector of Social Services, set down a marker for consumerist objectives:

- doing our best to fit services to the consumer's needs, not the consumer's needs to the service;
- making sure consumers have information about services and how to gain access to them;
- providing equal access to services, irrespective of race, sex and disability;
- giving as much choice as we possibly can to each individual or family;
- listening seriously to what consumers say about us and the services being offered or provided;
- responding as quickly as possible to requests for help, and minimising bureaucracy;
- involving consumers in decisions about their lives;
- giving consumers reasons for our decisions;
- treating complaints very seriously;
- making reception a comfortable, welcoming experience everywhere;
- meeting the needs of carers and listening to their wishes;
- creating an atmosphere of partnership in all that we do.

However, over subsequent years the implementation of such objectives has proved unusually difficult. Harding et al. (1993) report on a series of workshops held in 1991 between service users and service providers which sought to address some of the difficulties and suggest some solutions. These solutions include the development of user-led criteria for service users' involvement in service planning and delivery including eight key areas:

- involvement and the agency role;
- access to the agency or service;
- the extent of involvement;
- support and access for involvement;
- the nature of involvement;
- agency practice;
- agency policy for involvement;
- the effectiveness of involvement.

Opinions are still divided as to how much service user involvement is happening in practice. Morris (1994) is critical of advances made in this area, while Whiteley (1994) reports gradual developments. Philpott (1994) optimistically attributes to managers a key role in promoting such developments.

There are other indices of service users' power in relation to agencies. The service users' right to complain against an agency has been vigorously upheld by Cordern and Preston-Shoot (1987a). This right has been subsequently enshrined in both the Children Act (1989) and the NHS and Community Care Act (1990). Community care complaints procedures should have been in place within all local authorities since April 1991, but the effectiveness of these procedures remains considerably in doubt. George (1992) surveyed a highly-variable pattern of complaints procedures – sometimes centralised, sometimes more local – with differing criteria and varying methods of recording and registering complaints.

Service users also indicate that the processes of complaining can be off-putting:

> I didn't know who to complain to because they all appear as a Mafia organisation.

> They refused to acknowledge I have a complaint. (Thoburn, 1992, p. 71)

Moreover, social services users have not traditionally been quick to register complaints. George (1992) reports that in 1990–91, only 4 per cent of complaints to local authority ombudspersons concerned social services departments. Rees and Wallace (1982, p. 47) suggested that elderly people in particular make few complaints about the services they receive. If the reasons for such reluctance to complain include, as George (1992) suggests, the linguistic competence of the complainants and their knowledge of the complaints system, it is likely that complaints will remain at a low level.

It can be argued that for service users to make more use of complaints procedures a shift will be required in the attitude of agency workers and managers. Complaints made and responded to are a sign of an effective organisation which values the quality of its service and the response of service users, realistically recognises that services will not always be satisfactory and seeks to discover and remedy those occasions. Many workers and managers, however, are too inclined to view complaints as personal criticism and/or a likely obstacle to career progression.

There have also been instances when service users have used the legal process to gain redress against an agency. Marchant (1993) describes how, following the failure of a complaints system to secure the services required from an agency, the case was taken to judicial review, in which the judge ruled in favour of the service user and not the agency.

Questions to ask are:

Are the service users I am in contact with reasonably satisfied with my agency?

Is there anything I can do to improve their satisfaction?

Which service users are participating least in the various processes of the agency, including planning? What can I do to improve this?

Should any service users be pursuing their dissatisfactions beyond mentioning them to me? How can I assist them?

Three-way relationships within the triangle

There are three three-way relationships in this triangular working context:

- the agency in relation to the service user/worker;
- the worker in relation to the service user/agency;
- the service user in relation to the agency/worker.

The agency in relation to the service user/worker relationship

Johnson (1972) describes how, in a general way, the state provides, through the agency, the legitimacy and resources whereby workers are able to help service users. Many writers have indicated specific instances of the need for agencies to support their workers, both in policy and practice. Morrison (1990), for example, indicates the need for agencies to support workers in distress during their work with service users, while Fisher (1990) expects an agency commitment to back-up care management and Wood (1989/90) expects a specific approach to child sexual abuse. Parsloe and Stevenson (1993) recognise that for front-line workers to empower users, managers must empower those workers. Raynor and Vanstone (1994) report an interesting project in which one probation service endorsed a particularly effective intervention method between workers and service users.

Agencies can also reinforce the work between workers and service users through their policies and practices for supervision and training. Good, regular supervision can be particularly valuable when a worker has become, in some sense, stuck in their work with a service user, be it from an emotional or intellectual difficulty in proceeding. The more emotionally distant position and the different perspective that a manager can offer will often move the work on (see Chapter 3). Workers need regular in-service training to meet the changing service patterns derived from new legislation and evolving social needs. Agencies have a particular role in determining these training needs, especially when they are not specified and funded by central government: for example, through the Training Support Programme.

Francis (1993a) reports on some of the ways in which agencies can help white workers who experience difficulty in working with black service users give a better service, rather than attempting to transfer the service user to black colleagues. She quotes 'their white, liberal defensiveness' as a major reason given by Daphne Statham, NISW (National Institute for Social Work) Director, for this difficulty. Two solutions are: supervision or awareness training, in which white workers can address their fear or guilt; rigorous and well-researched guidelines and procedures which are sensitive to differences in culture and religion.

There are times, however, when the agency does not support the work between service user and worker. In their gender analysis of social service agencies, Davis and Brook (1985) indicate the likelihood of structural discrimination, which may arise between mainly male upper managers on the one hand and female workers and service users on the other. This is likely to be compounded by other structural differences, such as race. Frost and Stein (1989) indicate some of the campaigns which are addressing the ways agencies can support women working with women and black workers working with black service users.

To a degree, the more any worker becomes involved with the particular need experienced by a given service user, the further both of them become distanced from the bureaucratic operations of the agency. At times, the worker and service user may wish to form an alliance in order to influence the agency. Such an alliance goes beyond the familiar circumstances whereby workers advocate the interests of service users to agency managers, in competition with other workers and service users for limited resources. Frost and Stein (1989) recommend the value of unusual alliances which transcend traditional boundaries in counteracting many of the effects of a decade of Thatcherism on the welfare state, which persist into the 1990s.

One example of such an alliance occurred between one of the authors and the son-in-law of an older woman. An appropriately flexible arrangement for sharing the care of the older woman was not immediately available from the agency. The worker and the son-in-law, who was an influential member of the local community, agreed on arguments for an extension to existing provision and occasions on which the son-in-law could participate in putting these arguments, thus successfully obtaining the flexible service the older person required.

The worker in relation to the service user/agency

The evidence from consumer studies (Rees and Wallace, 1982) suggests that the major achievement of the worker is to give a human face in a service user's encounter with an otherwise faceless, bureaucratic organisation, and to offset the alienation and dissatisfaction which can stem from this encounter.

The worker can have a more ambiguous role in how much they inhibit or facilitate the service users' access to the full functioning of the agency. This may include how much they inform the service user of all the agency's relevant resources, policies and procedures; how much they encourage the service user to participate as fully as possible in the agency's decisionmaking processes, and how much they encourage the service user to exercise their rights in making a complaint against the agency or in looking at the agency's records.

Service users may also wish to complain to agency managers about their worker. It is incumbent on workers not to obstruct this process, having exhausted all means to satisfy the service users themselves. Likewise, agency managers need to be alert to such situations and not afraid to damage internal staff relationships temporarily to ensure a proper service. At times, disciplinary action may be necessary. As agencies begin to take their role as qualifying training organisations seriously (CCETSW, 1989b), they may need to consider policies on whether service users can refuse to see student social workers or not, much as training hospitals have done.

The service user in relation to the worker/agency

A strong alliance between a worker and their agency can at times be perceived by service users as an advantage – for example, when a worker's reassurances about a promised resource or a committed course of action are reinforced by individual agency managers or within an agency case conference or meeting. This alliance will also be welcomed by managers, so that they can ensure that general policies or specific decisions are being implemented. Workers will tend to welcome it when they seek the authority of the agency to underline their chosen course of action.

However, such an alliance will often be less welcome to service users. Managers and workers will often work in tandem, for example in joint visits or planning meetings, when the news they bear for service users is not good: perhaps the absence or even withdrawal of a much-needed resource or the decision to pursue a course of action to which the service user is opposed. The alliance can be particularly distressing when a service user witnesses the worker's apparent support for their situation evaporate in the presence of their manager, when the alliance may be based not so much on firm agreement but compliance to authority.

When the service users consider they are opposed by both worker and agency managers, they must have the right to increase the power of their case. Complaints systems exist in many agencies, including in social services and social work departments, following the NHS and Community Care Act (1990) and Children Act (1989). Internal complaints systems, however, have some deficiencies. As Marchant (1993) indicates, social services committees can overturn recommendations from complaints procedures. Moreover, the disability group RADAR's Project Officer, John Keep, claims that the complaints systems do not fully empower service users: 'It drains clients of all energy being involved in complaints procedures, even with our support' (Ivory, 1994, p. 22).

It would be interesting to investigate what proportion of complaints are upheld and whether that proportion is increasing in a climate of increased user empowerment.

Processes of gaining redress or reinforcing the service user's case which are totally independent of the agency and worker include the ombudsperson, legal processes and collective action through local or national pressure groups. There are still very few high-profile court cases pursued by service users (Ivory, 1994), and the proportion of social services department cases pursued by ombudspersons is still very small.

5   The work process

In Chapter 4, our focus in examining the process of working in social care has been on the three major participants at any one point in time. In this chapter, we will change the focus in two ways: we will follow the process through time, and we will widen the scope to include more than those three basic participants. The chronological sequence we will explore is that of the individual work task from start to finish. The additional participants include the multi-agency context within which much work occurs and the considerable network of friends, relatives, neighbours and different communities which surround the referred service user.

The literature on social work contains a number of attempts to divide the work process into a sequence of phases (Pincus and Minahan, 1973; Goldstein, 1973; Butrym, 1976; Compton and Galaway, 1979; Egan, 1982; Taylor and Devine, 1993). The Central Council for Education and Training in Social Work have also made two such attempts (CCETSW, 1989a, 1995). These writers seek to delineate different phases which are characterised by different functions, activities and skills. Phases identified include: contact, engagement, assessment, planning, contract, intervention, evaluation and termination. Similar phases have been delineated within other professions, for example 'diagnosis' and 'treatment' in medicine (Lippitt et al., 1958).

From our systemic perspective, there is one primary purpose in determining different phases and their functions. Primarily, it is a means of placing a given work task within a temporal context by asking questions such as:

> *At what point is the work on this particular need?*
> *What needs to be done* now *in order for this work to progress?*

A sense of progression *through* the work process – in other words, of temporal *pattern* (see Chapter 3) – helps give a sense of *purpose* at any given point. Howe (1987) is in no doubt that social workers should be systematic and structured in their practice, and that such ordered practice is generally more effective (Fischer, 1978). Furthermore, if we know the different aims of each phase in the work process, we are then well placed to answer subsequent questions, such as:

> *Who determines what goes on at different points in the work process?*
> *What can be done to ensure the service user has more control at different*
>   *points in the process?*

However, there have been other purposes in seeking to delineate different phases in the work process. The unitary models propounded by Pincus and Minahan (1973) and Goldstein (1973) had an evident purpose of providing a unifying analysis of all social work tasks and thus contributing to the integration and increased professional power of hitherto discrete specialisms (see Chapter 2).

More recently, central government publications have also delineated particular phases for political reasons. In *Working Together under the Children Act 1989* (Home Office et al., 1991), a number of phases in child protection are outlined, several of which specify activities crucial to identifying and eliminating risk ('immediate protection' and 'investigation') and ensuring inter-agency communication ('child protection conference'). The delineation of these phases in itself discharges, to some extent, the high level of accountability under which statutory agencies and government operate in the field of child protection.

In clarifying the practices of care management and assessment, the Social Services Inspectorate (DoH and Scottish Office, 1991b) have propounded seven key stages, two of which, 'assessing need' and 'care planning', carefully separate the identification of need from the identification of resources. This separation is crucial to the division between purchaser and provider, and hence to the government's political purpose of increased privatisation of welfare.

The eight phases

We have identified a sequence of eight phases, many of which coincide with those of previous writers: beginning, engaging, convening, assessing, planning, intervening, evaluating and ending. We have added one phase, 'convening', to the more usual list, because it emphasises the importance of interaction in the work process. Moreover, we have used verbs, which emphasise the nature of a *process*, rather than the more usual nouns ('assessment' etc.), which tend to reify processes as *things*. The sequence of eight phases is represented in Figure 5.1.

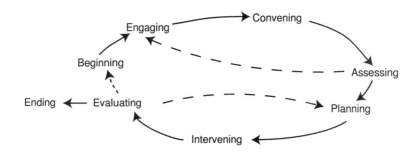

Figure 5.1 The social care process

However, a systemic approach is not only concerned with the delineation of different phases. It is also concerned with the relationship between the different phases.

The relationship between the phases

The continuous-line arrows in the diagram indicate a progression through the eight phases from beginning to ending. However, such orderly progression frequently does not occur, for four main reasons. First, any participant in the work process may wish to revisit an earlier phase before moving on to another phase (see the dotted-line arrows in the diagram). Consumer research into social work has indicated that worker and service user may part company after the assessment phase. The service user has presented one need, often practical, such as for the care of a dependent relative, and the worker is aware of, or more interested in, another need, perhaps an emotional one. At such times, worker and service user may have to re-engage in a common task.

A second reason why the process is not a straightforward progression through the phases is that, often, the phases themselves are not discrete but merged together. The process of assessing, for example, frequently entails intervening. The mere presence of a worker has an impact on the service user: perhaps an increased hope or fear or a sense of 'Here we go again!' In addition, many of the questions workers may ask in assessing – such as 'When did the need first arise?' – often lead the service user to an understanding which, in itself, may start a process of change.

While it is important to recognise that different phases can merge together, it can also be important, at other times, to make strenuous efforts to separate them. Complex bureaucratic agencies recognise that the entire work process with one specific social need will not necessarily be undertaken by the same staff in the same unit settings. The agencies have to determine between which phases transitions from one staff member or unit to another will occur. One common transition is from the start, when a referral is received by one staff member, to the subsequent stage of engaging and assessing, often performed by other staff. Another transition often occurs from short-term work, often of an assessment nature, to longer-term work, in which interventions will be guided by other staff. The division between purchasing (or assessing) and providing which has developed with the implementation of the NHS and Community Care Act (1990) has had a major impact within all sectors on the structural separation of different phases.

In statutory work, particularly, it is important to clarify when different phases begin or end. The Home Office et al. helpfully emphasise the importance of indicating *the end* of the investigation phase in child protection work when no grounds for concern have been revealed:

> Those with parental responsibility, the child (having regard to age, understanding and level of maturity) and the referrer, as appropriate, should be informed in writing. (Home Office et al., 1991, p. 30)

Such written indications can be one context marker (see Chapter 3) to mark a change in function on the part of the agency. Other context markers for this change which could prevent labelling and facilitate any further work with the families on a non-statutory basis might include a change of worker, setting or even agency.

More disappointing, however, is the apparent lack of emphasis in *Working Together under the Children Act 1989* (Home Office et al., 1991) on clearly designating *the start* of the investigation phase. The start is determined by the decision that the agency has 'reason to suspect that a child is suffering or likely to suffer significant harm' (Home Office et al., 1991, p. 28). This decision has major implications for the rights of parents and children, since investigations are sometimes conducted without the same regard for openness, sharing and participation as work with non-statutory functions. Since the decision has such major implications, it should, in our view, be clearly marked in some way – certainly within the agency – for example, on a standard form or by involving an agency manager as well as a social worker. This decision should also typically be communicated to those under investigation.

A third reason why an orderly progression through the phases may not occur is when key phases have to be omitted, permanently or temporarily. Situations of risk are often such occasions: a preliminary assessment of substantial risk can lead to an immediate intervention to protect, which only later may be followed by a more substantial assessment. In mental health work, the approved social worker who signs an order for compulsory assessment *intervenes* to remove the service user from a dangerous situation, and enables a subsequent assessment.

By identifying an early phase, 'immediate protection', and a later phase, 'comprehensive assessment', child protection procedures (Home Office et al., 1991) allow a similarly rapid movement to intervention. Such omissions are also commonplace in residential or day care settings, where workers have to act first to protect service users and ask questions later about why this adolescent or older person had become violent.

On other occasions, however, the pressure to proceed to an intervention without a fuller assessment or agreed plans may well need to be resisted. Social services and social work departments receive many referrals, for example stating that an older person should attend a day centre, receive meals on wheels or home care, or go into a residential home. These referrals are frequently made by well-intentioned doctors, health visitors, relatives or neighbours. However, all too often they lack any detailed information about needs or about the referred person's view of the proposed solution. Similar referrals are often received by private and voluntary agencies from statutory social workers. It is the responsibility of the agency receiving the referral to delay intervention and to ensure that due progression through the different phases occurs prior to intervening.

A final reason why the phases may not occur in orderly progression is that it is also possible for different participants in the process to disagree over exactly what phase they are in at a given time. The referrers mentioned above can see no reason for not proceeding rapidly to the intervening phase, while the agency receiving the referral will hopefully persuade them otherwise. Likewise, specialist fosterparents may be eager to start preparing a child for adoption ('intervening'), while the child may still want to settle into the foster placement ('engaging') after repeated disruptions to their life.

Timing is a key aspect to progression through the phases. Rees and Wallace (1982) report service users' dissatisfactions with the many delays to which they can be subject, as does Ivory (1994). Increased resources are more likely to diminish these than agency charters. These delays can result from the need to progress between staff with different functions within a large bureaucracy, or from work pressures. The Home Office et al. likewise indicate the need for speed in progressing through the different phases of work in child protection and yet warn of the dangers of undue haste:

> The potential for damage to the long-term future of the child by precipitate action must always be considered. (Home Office et al., 1991, p. 3)

Time can easily become a battleground during the work process. After inordinate delays before being seen, service users can suddenly find themselves being jostled along in uncomfortable haste towards an intervention which they have been unable to consider fully. Moreover, agency managers may put pressure on workers to speed up a pace of work with which workers and service users are content, because of additional work pressures.

Another important aspect of the progression through the phases is continuity. Rees and Wallace (1982) report that some service users, for example the parents of disabled offspring, find the lack of continuity in personnel far from helpful. The value of continuity in workers is also emphasised in the government guidelines on community care (DoH and Scottish Office, 1991a, p. 15). Yet, in direct contradiction, the very nature of the purchaser/provider split in community care encourages a discontinuity in sector, let alone in agency setting or individual worker.

Discontinuity, like delays, may also be a function of the workforce specialisation inherent in complex bureaucracies: a service user may be transferred from receptionist (customer service officer) to duty worker to short-term worker to long-term specialist.

Continuity can be greatly aided by appropriate recording. Within complex agencies in particular, key information from one phase often needs to be recorded so that other staff can pursue it at another. The written diaries kept in many residential establishments which communicate between shift-workers provide one example, as do the running records in fieldwork settings and the standardised forms related to distinct phases in the process, such as referral, assessing, planning, reviewing.

Recording not only serves to ensure some continuity between phases, it can also empower the service user's participation in the progress through the phases. First, the referred service user or their delegate can be actively involved in writing documents which mark key phases in the process. The DoH and Scottish Office (1991b, p. 39) suggest that many service users could participate in writing the referral, the assessment and the care plan entailed in delivering community care. Many fostering and adoption workers encourage prospective parents to write major sections of their assessments. In these ways, service users can not only ensure that they agree with the accounts made of them, but also that they are couched in language which does not exclude or alienate them (Lishman, 1994). Once opinions or decisions of a social services agency are recorded, they become available under the legislation and can become evidence in a service user's case for redress.

The context of the eight phases

The eight phases of working in social care occur within a context. Much happens before the beginning and after the ending. The worker's window into the service user's life is essentially brief and limited, even when service users experience social need throughout their lives through structural disadvantage or personal incapacity. It is quite likely that a service user or someone in their immediate network will have struggled to find ways of meeting a need long before it comes to the attention of a personal social services agency. It is equally likely that they will be beset by similar needs long after the social services agency has ended its contact. It is important, therefore, for agencies to be humble about their essentially partial influence on service users' lives.

Agencies have a responsibility to inform potential referrers and service users what services they can expect, so that they can decide whether to begin the work process or not. This responsibility has become a legal duty for local authorities under the Children Act (1988) and NHS and Community Care Act (1990). It is also a cornerstone of user empowerment, since 'information is power' (Family Rights Group, 1991, p. 10).

However, it is difficult to be optimistic that all necessary information will be conveyed. Previous legislation, such as the Chronically Sick and Disabled Persons Act (1969) and the Disabled Persons Act (1986), has placed similar duties upon local authorities, but to little avail.

Gathering useful information requires proper resources. Written information will need to be attractive, accessible and intelligible to a wide range of readers, including children, people with reading and other learning disabilities, and people whose first language is not English. It will need to reach its intended recipients in places they attend, such as post offices and local newspapers, and not just the reception desks of area offices or public libraries. It will need to include, as Neate (1991) suggests, information about the limitation of services, and it will need to be available in non-written form for people who cannot read, for example over the local radio station or on tape. It is difficult to imagine resourcing adequate to this task.

Another expensive task for social services agencies, prior to a specific work process, is to induct potential referrers into referral-making. Although this is generally not a statutory duty, it is a requirement of statutory agencies involved in child protection work (Home Office et al., 1991, p. 27). This task can be achieved through designated liaison workers, by giving referrers feedback about the appropriateness of their referrals, or through written guidelines for referrers.

Following the end of the process of working with an individual social need, the agency has a responsibility to monitor several aspects of that process. In planning community care, local authorities and their practitioners have a responsibility to monitor and respond to any perceived shortfall between the assessment of need and the current availability of resources – 'unmet need' (DoH and Scottish Office, 1991b, p. 66).

In the light of current low public opinion about the effectiveness of social care work, it would also be appropriate for agencies to collate and disseminate information about the success of their work. Research consistently suggests a high level of effectiveness in social work (Cheetham et al., 1992). Such information could provide some antidote to media images attacking social work and social services, and could be organised by bodies such as the Association of Directors in Social Services.

Beginning

The start is a particularly important phase in all enterprises, from infancy to opening ceremonies, and starting work in social care is no exception. It is important from our systemic perspective largely because it establishes a *pattern* (see Chapter 3) between participants, particularly concerning control.

A major feature of beginning is that everything is new. Given the unique and individual nature of social need (Payne, 1991), it could be argued that at the start, all participants in the endeavour of working with a particular social need are equally new to that endeavour. However, personal social services agencies and many of their staff will have considerable experience of similar work processes, while service users often have little or no prior experience of social care work, so they can be considerably disadvantaged in their ability to participate in setting appropriate patterns.

Becoming a service user – the first filter

Personal social services agencies are set up in order to meet social needs and employ workers for this purpose, but what brings someone experiencing a social need into contact with the agency? Phillips (1983) suggests that this is a much neglected subject of research, although it is better documented in mental health work (Goldberg and Huxley, 1980). There will be a number of filters which encourage or prevent people with social needs entering into a work process with an agency worker. Payne (1991, 1992) uses the phrase 'route to clienthood' to describe this process, and suggests that people possess three elements to start as clients, or service users:

- awareness of some issue as a problem;
- an impulsion towards receiving help;
- consciousness of the availability of the agency.

Payne's useful analysis suggests the important distinction between, on the one hand, the many people in the community who are aware of some issue as a need – Bradshaw's (1972) 'felt need' – and, on the other, the much smaller number who, for additional reasons, take that problem to a social care agency – 'expressed need'. Green (1988) indicates the very small proportions of carers who express need to social services departments. However, his analysis somewhat belies the considerable complexity of events and emotions which comprise this first filter in the work process, whereby service users or referrers approach an agency in order to start that work. Far from having an impulsion to receive help, many people become 'unwilling' service users when they are subject to the concerns of well-meaning, oversolicitous or even malicious relatives, neighbours or professionals.

Even 'willing' service users come to a social services agency with a wide range of emotions and expectations: trepidation in the face of authority and the media image of social work; foreboding based on their own or someone else's difficult experience; hope that a pressing problem may be alleviated; excitement that at last they have been set on the right path; embarrassment or shame that they have not met a need themselves. It is important that, at the start, the harmful effects of some of these emotions are diminished and the beneficial effects of others are enhanced.

Reception

It is often thought that the agency's starting point for work with a particular social need is the referral. In fact, there is invariably contact with a social services agency before a referral is taken. Invariably, the first contact with an agency is with 'reception', be it in person, by phone or by letter, and this is a frequently underestimated part of the whole process. In smaller, voluntary, private and statutory settings, this reception function is unlikely to be performed by a member of staff with that job description.

Service users of several caring professions attach considerable importance to their reception by the agency. Rees and Wallace (1982) report how some women, expecting a personal approach, are dissatisfied with the impersonality of being ignored and kept waiting, and how some service users' initial reactions at reception may well be carried forward into their later contact. Lishman (1994) also underlines the importance of reception.

In their consideration of delivering community care, the Social Services Inspectorate and the Scottish Social Work Service Group (DoH and Scottish Office, 1991b, p. 37) suggest that agencies should be *welcoming, positive, proactive* and *informed* in their response to new service users, in contrast to the findings of a much earlier survey (DHSS, 1978). Many social services agencies have undoubtedly responded to these suggestions and the general climate of consumerism: new reception areas have been designed, and many receptionists or 'customer services officers' have received the training advocated for community care (DoH and Scottish Office, 1991b, p. 38). However, it remains the exception that service users are invited to participate in planning agency reception areas, either through a simple questionnaire or through more complex agency–user planning processes.

Making a referral – the second filter

Most social care agencies distinguish an initial enquiry from the subsequent making of a referral. A referral is seen as the formal starting point of work between the agency and those outside it. This formality is usually observed through written recording, often on a standardised form through which the agency seeks to control the content. The referral can provide a significant contribution to the agency's statistical analysis of workload, and as such becomes an instrument for fulfilling accountability and for securing appropriate resources.

The referral is also the first substantial negotiation between the agency and those who use it. The referrer seeks to establish a legitimate area of work for the agency. The agency, for its part, will wish to ensure that the work is appropriate for the agency. Once this negotiation has taken place and is duly recorded, the written referral can become evidence in the service user's right of redress in the event of receiving an inadequate service.

The progress from enquiry to referral is thus a significant second filter. The literature suggests that service users have little power in determining their progression through this filter. Vickery (1981) reported a study of referrals of older people living at home and concluded that referrals were actively discouraged by agency workers if they did not conform to the workers' expectations of delivering a prescribed, practical service. Moreover, the DHSS study (1978) indicated that in hospital settings, the individual social worker had considerable power to determine when an informal chat became a formal referral.

Making a referral is clearly an important initial process in working in social care. None the less, the attitudes of workers and agencies frequently undermine this importance. The DHSS study (1978) found that social services agencies often delegated unqualified staff to perform this crucial task despite their lack of training. Despite increased proportions of qualified staff since then, such tendencies still persist, and unqualified community care practitioners often take referrals, while qualified social work staff may view the process of taking new referrals as distracting them from the more crucial job of processing existing work and worrying them with unfamiliar problems. These rather unhelpful attitudes can be seen as partly the result of the anxiety engendered by 'beginnings' (Butler and Elliott, 1985) in contrast with the relative comfort of familiar work, which is at a much later stage.

At the point of making a referral, the work process involves a minimal interaction between three participants: the referrer (who seeks to make the referral), the agency worker (who seeks to define, clarify and agree the referral on the agency's behalf) and the referee (the person whom the referrer defines as experiencing a social need). In the case of self-referrals, the interaction is simplified to two participants. However, statutory social services agencies and many voluntary and private agencies receive many referrals from people other than the referred person, and it is with these 'third-party' or 'indirect' referrals that difficulties can beset the work process from the start.

Third-party referrals raise many questions about the involvement of the referee, since they are potentially secretive communications behind the referee's back. At a very basic level, the agency needs to know whether the referee is aware that a referral is being made to this agency, and if so, exactly what they expect to be contained within it (Fisher, 1990). The agency also needs to know the level of agreement which the referee has towards the referral being made and its contents. If the referrer suggests that the referee is not aware, the agency needs to decide under what circumstances the referee should be made aware, and by whom. Some of these questions become explicit on an agency's standard referral form. Often, they do not.

The Social Services Inspectorate and Scottish Social Work Services Group make the interesting suggestion that:

> Many potential users and carers (or third parties) are able and willing to complete standard forms, thus saving staff time; it is only a minority who may require assistance. (DoH and Scottish Office, 1991b, p. 39)

While entirely laudable in its attempt to establish a genuine partnership between service user and agency at the outset, this suggestion somewhat overlooks the potential difficulties when the service user, carer and other professionals conflict. Moreover, it neglects the essential power issues between the agency and an outsider in determining whether a referral will be *taken* (by the agency) as well as *made* (by the referrer) and the precise details of that negotiation.

It is also interesting to explore the relative roles of social workers and their managers in accepting referrals. The DHSS study (1978) reported how referrals from councillors at that time were often received by agency managers. Later, the Home Office et al. (1991, p. 39), also made it clear that senior agency managers should be involved in referrals about organised abuse. These involvements seem to be largely due to the need to demonstrate overtly the agency's exercising of accountability. For the most part, however, accountability is devolved to basic-grade staff, who may negotiate referral-taking with first line managers. In many agencies, first line managers are required to sign forms indicating their agreement to referrals. This signature effectively underscores the extent to which the referral is an initial working contract between the agency (and not just one worker) and someone outside it.

Having discussed the *process* of referral-making, we will now turn to the potential *content* of referrals. If the basic interaction is between referrer, agency and referee, the referral will need to contain answers to the following questions about this interaction:

What does the referrer expect from the agency?
Why have they approached it at this particular time?
Does the referee, as far as the referrer knows, have an existing or past relation-
   ship with the agency?
Is the referee aware of the referrer's contact with this agency?
Is the referee in agreement with the referrer's contact?
What is the relationship between the referrer and the referee?
What is the referrer's view of the need experienced by the referee?
What are the grounds for the referrer's view?
What does the referrer think the referee's view is of the need they are
   experiencing?
What is the referrer's view of a potential way of meeting the need?
Is the referrer aware of any other special needs on the part of the referee which
   the agency should know in pursuing the referral, for example irregular or
   difficult accessibility, language problems, communication disabilities?

A referral has been usefully likened to the loose thread of a tangled ball of wool (Palazzoli, 1984). If the thread is pulled carefully, the complex interactions which often surround and perpetuate social need start to be unravelled, and this process is aided by asking questions of this sort.

Allocation – the third filter

Once a referral has been agreed by the agency, the next step (or filter) is the decision to allocate the work for a given worker to pursue. Not all referrals are allocated, and two questions are:

Who determines whether they are allocated?
What are the criteria for such decisions?

With the implementation of the NHS and Community Care Act (1990), social services departments are instituting 'eligibility criteria' which are communicated to staff and, in some cases, service users. Ivory (1994) suggests that, in part at least, these criteria should be very strict, in order to minimise the occurrence of 'unmet need'.

Team leaders often play a major role in this decision, either as individuals or as part of a team process. Team processes can respond sensitively not only to agency policy through the team leader, but also to the more detailed knowledge of the team member who took the referral, and the experience of other team members.

Needless to say, the referrer or referee will have considerably less power to influence the decision, except in the manner of making the referral and through persistent enquiry about allocation. Indeed, many referrers and referees will be unaware of this additional process, although a thorough referral-taker will inform the referrer of it.

However, the power of the referrer would be considerably enhanced if they were informed not only of the process but also of the criteria for allocation. These eligibility criteria are often covert and not publicised. The Social Services Inspectorate and Scottish Social Work Services Group suggest a number of criteria for allocating community care referrals, including:

- severity or complexity of needs;
- degree of risk or vulnerability of user or carers;
- degree of stress experienced by the user, carers or other agencies;
- length of time already spent on a waiting list. (DoH and Scottish Office, 1991b, p. 43–4)

If these or similar criteria were made overt for the social needs of all service user groups and communicated to referrers and referees, they would have a right of redress if the criteria were not upheld.

Another important aspect of the decision to allocate is the choice of worker to whom the referral is allocated. Guidance on community care allocation concerns, in particular, the nature and complexity of the assessment required, and hence the expertise of the worker making the assessment (DoH and Scottish Office 1991b, p. 42). Agencies and workers are also becoming alert to the fact that anti-oppressive practice can be fostered in the allocation of a worker. Sexually abused girls and women suffering violence are only two examples of instances when female service users may request female workers. Black service users may also request black workers. Orthodox Turkish and Asian women may often prefer female workers (Virdee, 1992). This is not merely a matter of idiosyncratic personal preference, but a necessary decision to combat strong institutional disadvantage.

Engaging

Once it has been established that a given piece of work is starting, worker and service user, and perhaps many other people, will need to engage in the work process. This is a preliminary phase, during which a relationship is formed which facilitates later stages of the work. This relationship has two main aspects to it: human and work-related. The human aspect has been discussed in some detail in Chapter 4. We shall concentrate here on the work-related aspects.

Central among these work-related aspects is the clarification of expectations about the work which is to be undertaken. Sainsbury (1983) reports that many service users were uneasy and confused by a lack of clarity about why workers had visited them. Corby (1992) also suggests that service users prefer workers to let them know honestly where they stand, rather than hedging their purposes about with vagueness. Whether the work to be embarked upon is statutory or voluntary, it is incumbent upon the worker to state the nature of a third-party referral which has initiated this work, and to clarify the service user's view of that referral. Even in the case of a self-referral, the worker should clarify whether the service user's view at this time has remained the same as it was when the referral was made. Without clarity of expectation and purpose, the clash of perspectives noted by Mayer and Timms (1970) and Davies (1985) is more likely to undermine future work.

Another important work-related aspect of the initial relationship is the service user's attitude to the agency and/or the worker. Sometimes, the service user will have had prior contact with the agency: information about this is often readily available in agency records. The worker may have to preface this new piece of work with a review of past work with the agency. Often, the service user has heard about the agency from another service user and may well have preconceived ideas about how the service may be provided, for better or worse. Invariably, the service user will have images of personal social services agencies and their workers drawn from the media. Old and young alike may well fear that a visit from a statutory agency social worker presages a removal from their own home against their will. Many of these preconceptions will only be hinted at in conversation, and workers need to be alert and proactive in their attempts to tackle them.

The need to ensure a level of relaxed exchange and to clarify the purposes of an initial contact remain every bit as important in statutory work. Smith (1991) and the Home Office et al. (1991) both describe the importance of helping the child relax and establishing an initial rapport between worker and child in child protection work. Likewise, it would seem crucial, in the interests of service users' rights and the overriding importance of honesty in public dealings, that workers should clarify at the onset the statutory nature of their work, if applicable, rather than seek to veil it with obfuscation. If workers seek to conceal their purposes for fear of violence from service users, then agencies should offer the protection of co-work, electronic communication or the police, rather than covertly encouraging workers to be less than clear about their purposes.

Agencies have other parts to play in the processes of engaging. Reception areas and interviewing rooms are more likely to be user-friendly if they are light, bright and comfortably furnished. Agencies should also provide the materials which help service users relax and feel less at a disadvantage: play materials for children of all cultures; relaxing literature in appropriate languages and likely to be of interest to working-class service users, and not just the cast-off magazines of mainly middle-class agency staff; the opportunity to buy a drink and to change a baby's nappy. Agencies can also encourage workers to make the home visits which set many service users at ease and empower them to explain their situation most effectively (Jordan, 1975).

Beyond these material provisions, agencies have it in their power to do much to encourage an ethos within which workers and service users can engage in a working relationship. The increasing 'task orientation' within a climate of managerialism can be tempered with a 'people orientation', which recognises that people have needs beyond simply being pushed through the work process with undue haste. Similarly, rising workload pressures which force workers to gallop in and out of service users' lives in their haste to move on to the next task can perhaps be reduced through more active workload prioritisation, in order to create the time for a more relaxed human encounter with service users.

More often than not, the worker needs to engage with a number of people in addressing one particular social need. However, this is not always a simple process: the different people may be in considerable conflict, and establishing a working relationship with one may jeopardise that process with another. Moreover, widening the network for engagement may introduce a level of complexity, or even a threatened loss of control, which the worker may not welcome. The following guidelines are offered to help the worker in such circumstances:

- Clarify, in conjunction with the referrer and referee, who are the people with whom you may need to establish a working relationship.
- Recognise that you may need to engage with these people gradually; one at a time, or in different combinations.
- Be wary of forming a premature alliance with one person before even engaging with another who may be opposed to them, for example beginning intensive work with a custodial parent before meeting a non-custodial parent.
- Recognise that sometimes, because of conflict or distance, it is not possible to engage with everyone indicated. If there is conflict between people, even if it is your purpose to help those with *less* power, it is usually better to engage initially with those who have *more* power – for example, parents rather than children; officers in a residential home rather than junior staff; a younger householder rather than the older relative who lives with them. Of course, if you are using your own statutory power, it may overcome the power differentials between service users.
- Listen to the perceptions of the problem of as many relevant people as possible. This includes refusing to accept the way some service users

will attempt to disqualify others as 'nosey' neighbours, 'unhelpful' or 'incompetent' professionals, 'young' or 'old' people.

Example

The following example shows how a worker can gradually engage with a number of people in attempting to meet a particular need.

Following a social services department referral by a daughter expressing concern for her mother because her (paternal) grandmother had 'her knife into the whole family', the allocated worker wrote to the daughter attempting to clarify the situation. The mother then phoned the worker to explain her point of view directly. The worker arranged to meet the mother and her husband at the worker's office, and worked out with them how to present their current difficulties to the grandmother. The next meeting was at the service users' home with mother, father and grandmother, at which grandmother was invited to explain her view of current difficulties. At a slightly later stage, two daughters, including the initial referrer, were invited to a meeting and encouraged to play a part in resolving the difficulties.

Two significant people with whom the worker failed to engage in this instance were the grandmother's health visitor and GP, although the oversight was not harmful. While the health visitor was advocating short-stay breaks for the grandmother as the only solution to the family's relationship conflicts, the more powerful GP and the social worker were both separately urging the father to decide whom he supported when his wife and his mother were arguing, and not to sit on the fence – an approach which seemed to pay dividends.

However, the need for workers in one social services agency to engage with the workers of other agencies in resolving service users' needs cannot be overstated. The human aspects of these inter-agency working relationships have become somewhat neglected under the pressures of financial cuts. Regular meetings between social workers and health visitors, for example, seem to be largely a thing of the past, although community care initiatives are increasingly bringing health and social services workers together. However, workers from different agencies will often meet or communicate by phone to clarify their purposes before making a joint assessment visit.

Agencies can also assist in this process by supporting joint training for these workers which helps to establish agreed work methods and dismantle long-standing inter-agency rivalries and misconceptions. This has proved successful between police and social workers in child protection and could well be a similarly successful strategy for health and social workers in community care practices.

Convening

Convening entails bringing together in the same place a number of people who have a significant part to play in meeting a particular social need. By virtue of being together, people can often share and create ideas and resolve differences in a way that is less easy to achieve when acting in isolation, or with the more limited interaction of phone calls or letters. Convening is therefore of particular importance in a systemic approach.

The importance of bringing significant people together has been recognised for some time. Ever since the Maria Colwell Inquiry (Colwell Report, 1974), case conferences have formed a major strategy in inter-agency co-operation for the protection of children. In family therapy and networking practice, the processes of convening have for some time received special emphasis (Teismann, 1980; Stanton and Todd, 1981; Carpenter and Treacher, 1983). Furthermore, with the increased inter-agency and worker–service user partnerships entailed in the Children Act (1989) and NHS and Community Care Act (1990), it is likely that convening will become an increasingly important process. Family group conferences (Morris, 1994) may increase in popularity and will require convening.

Convening is, in our view, a significantly influential process in itself to warrant being conceived of as a distinct phase in the work process. Indeed, this is how the child protection conference is currently viewed (Home Office et al., 1991, p. 26). However, convening often plays a major part in increasing the effectiveness of other phases. Thus the child protection conference and other statutory conferences and review meetings can often aid joint assessment, planning and intervention. In both statutory and voluntary contexts, the process of convening a wider network can, as Dimmock and Dungworth (1985) suggest, produce a 'network effect' which constitutes the principal intervention to meet a given need.

However, larger meetings can often shift the balance of power further away from service users. King cites the response of a woman to joint mental health planning meetings:

> When I first attended the meetings there were all these people coming in with filo-faxes and I panicked. (King, 1991, p. 17)

Another woman complained of the same meetings:

> It's a very intimidating situation. I feel as though I might say something stupid and often . . . it just goes over my head. (King, 1991, p. 18)

Thoburn cites a similar response:

> I had things to say, but I didn't get a chance. I did try to say one thing and I was jumped on by the chair officer. (Thoburn, 1992, p. 69)

The DoH and Scottish Office (1991b, p. 83) also recognise the intimidating nature of these large meetings.

Three major principles can help prevent service users being significantly disadvantaged in such meetings. First, the number of participants in the meeting should be limited to the minimum necessary to achieve the work: what Skynner (1971) usefully termed the 'minimum sufficient network'. This reduces the risk of overpowering service users by the sheer weight of numbers.

Second, workers and other agency staff should attend to the important details which empower service users at such gatherings (Driscoll and Evans, 1992): not patronising or otherwise undermining their contributions; arranging the meetings at a time and place which suit service users as much as workers and managers; avoiding treating service users as second-class participants by welcoming and introducing them in a similar manner to workers; ensuring they have all necessary support in communicating their views adequately, for example an interpreter, signer, advocate or supportive friend who is of an appropriate gender or ethnic origin (Virdee, 1992). All these details stem from a fundamental value base which holds that service users bring a unique and crucial perspective to the social needs which they alone experience.

A final, related principle is that equal if not greater emphasis should be placed on convening the networks which surround the *service user*. All too often, emphasis is on convening the network which surrounds the *worker*, which increases the power of the worker and the agency. Many meetings convened by social services departments, for example, are likely to comprise at least two or three workers from different settings or disciplines, their immediate line manager(s), a departmental chair and possibly an administrative minute-taker before any service users are involved, let alone their friends, relatives, neighbours and others with common interests. In order to ensure that the service users' networks are accorded due significance, workers and their agencies will need to recognise their considerable strengths and resources. The family group conferences enshrined in the New Zealand Children, Young Persons and their Families Act (1989) and increasingly promoted for the UK achieve this redistribution of power.

Example

Mrs Jones had several of her children removed from her care and was in considerable, sometimes violent, conflict with her two remaining teenage daughters. The three of them lived in a supportive neighbourhood on a working-class council housing estate. On one occasion, Mrs Jones was seriously considering whether one of the girls would have to be taken into care by the local authority. However, the neighbourhood was concerned to avoid this, and a neighbourhood meeting was convened, involving family, neighbours and a social worker, at which several plans were agreed which effectively eliminated this need. Since many of the neighbours were suspicious of statutory social work agencies, the meeting was convened by a highly-motivated neighbour.

Guidelines

The following are some guidelines on how to convene a wide range of different gatherings:

- *Decide in consultation with others, who are the significant people who need to be brought together.* Service users will frequently have a clear sense of the people who are having most impact on a social need, and managers can often advise over other related agencies and workers.
- *Take personal responsibility for ensuring that the gathering is convened.* Relevant people will not automatically gather together – even family members, if it is seen as in some sense a 'family problem'. The worker needs to take the responsibility of ensuring that the gathering is convened, even if they do not convene it themselves.
- *Decide, with others, who is most likely to convene the gathering successfully.* Sometimes, the power of the worker within a statutory social services agency may be sufficient to convene all the significant people. At other times, a service user who is particularly motivated to meet the need may be better placed to influence their relative or neighbour to attend, or a worker from another agency may have a better relationship with a service user and thus be better placed to invite them.
- *Clarify an appropriate rationale for everyone to be at the gathering.* Gatherings of this sort can sometimes be seen as daunting, irrelevant or time-wasting. The fact that the worker or someone else wants them there may not be a sufficient reason for many people to overcome such obstacles. Different people may need a different rationale for attending the same gathering – one which fits their particular frame of reference or even their job specification.
- *Investigate and resolve the reasons why significant people do not wish to attend.* It is easy for a worker to misconstrue the reasons why, for example, a rather irritable resident may not attend a residents' meeting or a male partner may not attend a family meeting. If asked, the resident may express their discomfort in the presence of another resident, and the male partner may cite their shiftwork pattern. The worker can then respect the reasons, alter the conditions for the meeting or stress the rationale for that person's presence.

Assessing

Assessing occupies a pivotal place among all the phases in the work process. Its aim is to achieve an understanding of the nature of the social need, including some causal explanation. It is thus the foundation upon which solutions will be built. Moreover, it has been well established in the history of working with social need. Richmond (1917) is echoed by Sainsbury (1970) in stressing the central role of 'social diagnosis', as they named it, in social work. More recently, Davies asserts that:

> Assessment is the key to all good social work. (Davies, 1985, p. 156)

Since the 1970s, assessment has increasingly been consolidated as a major function within the practices of personal social services agencies and within wider social policy. Specialist assessment units and personnel have been established for a wide range of service user groups. Legislation has imposed a duty on local authorities to provide a comprehensive assessment for disabled people (Disabled Persons Act, 1986) and has given them the power to gain access in order to assess children at risk (Children Act, 1989).

The NHS and Community Care Act (1990) has taken this process still further. Not only has assessment been identified as a major, discrete process in delivering community care and established as a duty for local authorities, but it has also been recognised by the Social Services Inspectorate (DoH and Scottish Office, 1991a) as a specialism requiring considerable extra resourcing. Resourcing implications have, we suspect, become a major reason for specifying different levels of assessment which, in turn, require different degrees of specialisation and training. This has led to a politically-inspired additional phase being introduced into the work process:

> determining the level of assessment. (DoH and Scottish Office, 1991c, pp. 3–5)

It is to be hoped that such a delineation of levels will not become the strategic means for perpetuating the second-class service frequently delivered in the past to older people through a largely unqualified workforce (Rowlings, 1981).

The processes of assessment

While assessment can be identified as a discrete phase, it is by no means a single, undifferentiated process. Figure 5.2 indicates the possible interaction of a number of different processes.

Hypothesis is something of a jargon term, suggesting the formal process of hypothesis-testing which is the basis of scientific method. In fact, we have in

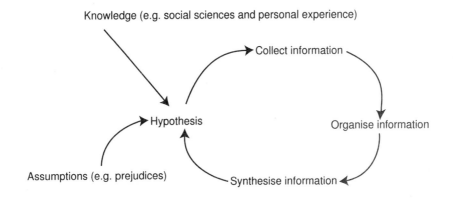

Figure 5.2 Assessment processes

mind the much less daunting process of forming a tentative or provisional explanation for the given social need. We suggest that such explanations help both service users and workers weed out the relevant information from the mass of irrelevant information. Our experience of training students and qualified workers suggests that the 'scatter-gun' approach mentioned by Coulshed (1991, p. 27), which often generates much irrelevant information, can be avoided by forming and testing hypotheses. However, hypotheses can only guide an assessment effectively if people are willing to abandon them on receiving information which disproves them.

Collecting and *organising* information are interrelated but different processes. Information can be organised before or after collecting. The assessment areas for child protection (DoH, 1988) and community care (DoH and Scottish Office, 1991b, pp. 58–9) provide structures for collecting and assembling information which are of the same order as the simpler checklists used by many experienced workers, although more complex. Smale et al. (1993) propose a model of assessment in which information is exchanged between worker and service user, and not merely uni-directionally.

Synthesising is the process of bringing together often divergent ideas to form one coherent picture. This is a particularly important process within a systemic approach which seeks to discover the patterns which connect apparently separate phenomena. Glaser et al. (1984) describe a model of bringing together many different pieces of information about a family. The process is akin to focusing a lens on the major or predominant themes. Butler and Elliott (1985) provide a number of general themes – for example, loss, material deprivation – which are often the synthesising focus of many complex social needs.

Assessing needs and resources

Community care policy clearly differentiates the assessment of need from the provision of resources. Its political aim is the increased privatisation of welfare, while its rhetoric is the promise of more responsive services:

> If services are to be made more responsive, it is necessary to identify the disparity between assessed needs and currently available services. This is most effectively achieved where the responsibility for assessing need is separated from that of delivering or managing services. (DoH and Scottish Office, 1991a, p. 7)

Undeniably, a concentration on resources can be to the detriment of defining need. Social services departments receive many referrals from GPs, health visitors and others which request resources but do not specify need. Ahmad (1992) suggests that the lack of resources for black people can lead to the further disadvantage of a restricted assessment of need. Moreover, the requirement to ration scarce resources can discriminate against the needs of certain groups, such as black elders (Jadeja and Singh, 1993).

However, there are dangers in attempting to separate need completely from resource. Concentrating solely on need can lead to unrealistic expectations, since even some most basic material needs – for money, employment, housing, food – are not being met by the current allocation of limited resources (Holman, 1993).

Furthermore, need and resource are not so easily separated. 'Need' is a transitive verb which requires an object: 'I need . . . a cup of tea.' It is thus difficult to identify the process of 'needing' without also identifying the object of that need. As Morrison (1988) claims, there is a tendency for 'people to want what they know rather than know what they want'. It is only through the artificial intricacies of grammar that we can talk of 'a need' as though it were a *thing* in itself, rather than what it really is, a *process* of wanting or requiring something. Quite often, service users have spent a lot of time and energy seeking to identify exactly what it is they need, having spoken to neighbours, friends, relatives and other professionals.

There is also a sense in which assessing involves matching need with resource. Doing a jigsaw involves fitting the shape of the piece to the shape of the gap. Meeting social need is more complex and dynamic, of course, than doing jigsaws. However, a similar process occurs when a bereaved older woman, seeking to resolve her loneliness, discovers that the two or three different day centres and voluntary visitors that her worker suggests do not alleviate her loneliness, but that a long visit to her sister and a new gas fire for the cheerless nights do.

Service users will often wish to participate in assessing a proposed resource in order to check whether it fits or matches their need. Coulshed

(1991, p. 35) suggests a list of criteria for service users to use in assessing the suitability of a residential home: choice, rights, independence, privacy, dignity, fulfilment. Children in care will wish to assess substitute families carefully for their match with innumerable, poorly-defined but crucial criteria which the most skilled adoption and fostering workers have not perceived. The breakdown of an apparently ideal match may well reveal needs which have hitherto been hidden or inaccurately assessed.

When assessing need, it is also important to discover what solutions have been attempted in the past. Workers and service users must learn what has not worked, and why not, before planning new solutions. Sometimes, attempted 'solutions', such as alcohol abuse, have caused new problems. At other times, the attempted solution has actually helped to maintain the initial need (Watzlawick et al., 1974) – for example, when children prefer a reprimand or smack to no attention at all, and thus continue their attention-seeking behaviour.

Who determines the assessment?

Sainsbury (1970) and Coulshed (1988) describe assessment as a process whereby both worker and service user contribute with equal weight. Such a model of partnership requests a considerable shift in power from the paradigm of professionalism wherein expert workers determine needs through their own skill and knowledge and with little contribution from lay service users.

However, the model of equal partnership in assessment is a somewhat cosy one and disguises the possibilities of conflict between worker and service user. Consumer studies suggest there is less likelihood of such conflict when assessed needs are immediate and practical (Sainsbury et al., 1982); but conflict is more likely to arise in the assessment of interpersonal needs. Service users will often indicate a cause which is external to themselves ('the child'), while workers will often include the service user in their definition of the need ('parental handling').

When disagreements of this sort arise between workers and service users, the reported dissatisfaction of service users suggests that the perceived power of the workers predominates (Rees and Wallace, 1982, p. 60; Cordern and Preston-Shoot, 1987a). Ahmad (1992) doubts that white workers will respond constructively to black users who challenge their assessment. Moreover, Ellis (1993) suggests that professional power is often covert and difficult to challenge in such circumstances.

How can the power of service users be increased in assessing problems? One basic method is to maximise their participation in the assessment process. The Children Act (1989) promotes the principle that the child's views should be taken into account in the light of their age and understanding. Community care policy advocates encouraging service users 'to partici-pate to the limit of their capacity' (DoH and Scottish Office, 1991b, p. 51). This requires that interpreters are made available for users for whom English is not their first language, and that advocates are made available for those who are unable to present their view with clarity due to mental, physical or linguistic impairment.

Another method is to give due weight to the needs that service users them-selves present. Consumer studies indicate that:

> Practitioners should take seriously and treat with respect the problems presented to them. (Cordern and Preston-Shoot, 1987a, p. 18)

Biehal (1993) describes some of the obstacles to an accurate perception of service users' needs and some of the practice skills required to obviate them. However, the debate about the relative weight of service users' pre-sented needs and workers' perceived needs has a long history (Sainsbury, 1983, p. 3).

More recently, the debate has shifted to the possibility of self-assessment by service users. There is evidence (Neate, 1991) that less complex commu-nity care assessments can be completed by service users alone. Moreover, for some time now, prospective fostering and adoptive parents have been asked to complete major sections of the BAAF Form F by workers who wish to give them greater power in assessment. Children, too, can be asked to assess themselves through appropriate methods (Coulshed, 1991, p. 30).

However, any process of self-assessment is likely to be hedged around with limitations. Sometimes it is the way that a service user defines their need that perpetuates it: it takes someone else to help the service user to see it dif-ferently. For example, a home care assistant can persuade an older person that it is not their daughter's indifference which prevents her phoning regu-larly, but merely her hectic employment and family life.

More often, however, it will be the social services agency which seeks to impose limitations on the service users' capacity to define their own need. This occurs particularly when the agency is accountable either for the safety of vulnerable people or for the allocation of limited resources. Agencies usually exercise this power when managers have a key role in assessment decisions – for example, chairing panels and conferences which reach assess-ment judgements or constructing and applying eligibility criteria.

Multi-worker assessment

There is also a value in involving more than one worker in assessments. This can increase the reliability of the judgements being made: if two or more people say 'X is the case', X is more likely to be the case. Bateson (1973) compares the value of double description with the advantage of binocular vision over a one-eyed approach.

A second advantage of more than one worker contributing to an assessment stems from the different perspectives workers have. Different workers will perceive different things, and not simply confirm the same views. Workers' different perceptions stem from their different knowledge bases and from their varying assumptions and values. Sometimes, the differences can be mutually enhancing when, for example, one worker is more alert to a service users' material deprivation and another to their emotional stress. At other times, these differences can lead to conflicting explanations of the same phenomena: a woman's depression might be explained by structural discrimination, lack of support, the burdens of child rearing, hormones, internalised anger, and so on.

Within the same social care agency, two workers may often work together to assess a service users' needs (see Chapter 3). The co-work team may combine the different perspectives of: a worker and a manager; a social worker and a worker from another discipline, such as an occupational therapist; a field worker and a residential worker; a man and a woman, for example in child sexual abuse work (Barber, 1991) or marital work. Sometimes, the co-work team can be formed to reinforce similar perceptions born of similar work styles and methods, such as family therapy or group work (Dowling, 1979; Latham, 1982).

The number of workers involved may also be extended to include a whole team. Many teams in different settings – for example, a duty team or a patch team – collaborate in assessment on an informal basis. In some settings, such as residential or day care, the contribution of the team is more formally structured. All members of the team will contribute their view of the service user, sometimes from different perspectives, such as education, training, care, domestic or outreach.

Inter-agency co-operation in assessment is also increasing. The advantages of such co-operation are twofold: the greater difference of perspective between different professions; the discharging within one shared activity of the different functions for which different agencies are responsible. Thus, when a police worker and a social worker join together in a child protection assessment, not only are their different skills and knowledge combined but also their agencies' different responsibilities to investigate crime and prevent significant harm to children, thus preventing a potentially harmful duplication of assessment processes.

Inter-agency partnership in assessment is increasingly urged for child protection (DoH, 1991) and community care (DoH and Scottish Office, 1991c). Gibson and Robertson (1988) suggest that inter-agency work can enhance co-operation, but provide no analysis of inhibiting power differentials, particularly between social services workers and medical workers. CCETSW/

IAMWH (1989) warn of the difficulties social workers can experience in making a distinctive contribution in mental health assessments. The NHS and Community Care Act (1990) imposes a duty on local authorities to co-ordinate community care assessment, including medical opinion. It remains to be seen whether this status will increase the power of social services department workers in inter-agency assessments at a practice level.

It is often claimed that unhelpful differences of perspective, particularly of attitude, can be diminished by joint training and team-building (DoH, 1988). However, there is evidence that such training can, at times, reinforce stereotypes (Funnell et al., 1992). Moreover, there is a limit to how much agencies would wish to erode their differences. It can be argued that different agencies owe their existence within the state infrastructure to the perception that they are performing important and different functions. An excessive erosion of boundaries would thus jeopardise the continued existence of some agencies and professions.

Perhaps the greatest potential sufferer when workers of the same or different agencies combine in the process of assessing is the service user themself. Once workers have worked hard to achieve an agreement, it is possible that the sheer number of workers will overpower the opinion of the service user.

Assessing patterns

A systemic approach is not just concerned with the contribution of different participants in the process of assessing. It is also orientated towards the content of that assessment. An action-orientated assessment will often focus on individuals, their characteristics and behaviours. Community care policy provides a guideline for a comprehensive assessment of both service users and carers, which concentrates heavily on these two individuals but contains little about their relationship (DoH and Scottish Office, 1991b, pp. 58–9). There is also a danger that the permanent focus on the welfare of the child within the Children Act (1989) will encourage a similar concentration on the individual and on specific, isolated behaviours. We would argue that an assessment of significant harm to a child will require not only an investigation of the child and their environment, but also of the child *in relation to* their environment.

A systemic assessment focuses particularly on pattern (see Chapter 3) – the connections between apparently discrete events. When looking up at the cloudless night sky, most people see chaos; when astronomers look up, they see constellations. When looking at social need, we are concerned not only with the pattern of how the need connects with other circumstances *at one point in time*, but also how it connects *through time* with its start, its various changes and repetitions. In a lifetime of systemic study, Bateson (1973, 1979) sums these up with the phrase 'the pattern that connects'.

Patterns at one point in time – relationships

'Relationship' is the term which best describes the patterns which connect at one point in time. The human relationship at the centre of community care policy involves the service user and their carer. Caring can be described as a *complementary* relationship, in which one cares and the other is cared for. Some relationships between older, disabled people and those they live with, however, can be characterised as *symmetrical*, in that both aspire to the same position: of being cared for, of running the household. Of course, many relationships will adopt a mixed pattern: at times fitting into different, matching positions, at others vying for the same position (Bateson, 1973; Burnham, 1986).

There are other important features of human relationships. One is the degree of emotional closeness or distance between people: what Minuchin (1974) terms, respectively, 'enmeshment' and 'disengagement'. This is particularly evident in the extent to which one person responds to the emotions of another. Most relationships ebb and flow in their degree of emotional closeness without being problematic. Sometimes, however, problems arise because people are too close or too distant for the task at hand. A serious illness will require a level of closeness from those at hand. An adolescent offspring, on the other hand, may find it difficult to establish an independent life if they or their parents still seek to maintain a very close relationship.

A second important feature is how much the relationship is affiliative or oppositional. An affiliative relationship is characterised by loving, caring, sympathetic emotions, while an oppositional one is conflictual and angry. As with closeness/distance, there is a continuum from very affiliative to very oppositional.

Closeness and affiliation are not the same. Affiliative emotions can be rather cool, just as oppositional emotions can be extreme and intense. It is likely that the most dangerous relationships for vulnerable young children or older people are those which are very close and very oppositional (see Figure 5.3).

	Affiliative	**Oppositional**
Close		Most dangerous
Distant	Least dangerous	

Figure 5.3   Degrees of closeness and affiliation

Relationships also vary in the consistency of their patterning. Skynner (1982) describes a continuum of consistency from chaotic through rigid to flexible, in which he sees chaotic as worst and flexible as best. Thus, within the community care service user–carer relationship, a chaotic pattern is one in which there is no obvious pattern of who cares for whom; a rigid pattern exists when only one person ever cares for the other no matter what happens, while a flexible pattern allows for variations if, for example, a chronically disabled person will care for an able-bodied but acutely sick partner. However, Skynner (1982) seems to be unaware that the pattern completes a circle (see Figure 5.4), since flexibility can easily tip back into chaos.

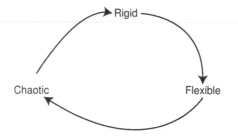

Figure 5.4   Consistency of patterning

A crucial dimension in relationships is the distribution of power: the extent to which one person can influence the other. People derive power both personally – through their physical strength, knowledge and characteristics such as ambition, aggression, perseverance – and also structurally, through their ascribed status and role within wider society and organisations. It is rare that one person wields all the power in a relationship. Moreover, the distribution of power within a relationship can be highly complex – for example, when a frail, intelligent, female, black care assistant in a children's home confronts a large, muscular, white, adolescent male resident with learning disability.

Thus far, we have concentrated on two-way relationships. However, social care usually takes place in more complex contexts, and it is necessary to understand the nature of wider relationship patterns. Two common patterns are alliances and coalitions. Alliances are formed when two or more people come together in order to achieve a common aim. A coalition has the additional component that the aim is to the detriment of another person, and that it is often pursued in a rather underhand or secretive way. Coalitions are often most damaging when they run counter to expected alliances – for example, when a residential care officer and a resident combine forces to undermine another officer.

Another common pattern in more complex relationships is scapegoating, when one person is blamed as the cause of the distress or discomfort that other people are suffering. Often, the victim of scapegoating can be clearly identified as different, for example through skin colour or gender, and appreciates and reinforces that difference, although not the way in which it is treated. The authors have known several stressed social work teams in which a black, male manager has been seen as the primary cause of that stress by predominantly white, female workers.

Patterns in communication are often seen as a significant indicator of how relationships function. Certain patterns in the processes of communication can speak volumes, while the content does not. For example, a case conference can start in an ordered fashion with the chair asking each participant in turn to state their perspective. After a while, however, it may become apparent that two participants are in conflict: they may speak at the same time as if eager to silence each other; the one may always follow the other, as if activated by the opposite view which they must repudiate; they may abandon the device of speaking or responding to the chairperson, a device which can effectively diffuse conflict through a third party. It is not just what they say – their words and their tone – but also the sequence – overlapping, one after the other, not speaking through the chair – which indicates the conflict.

Another significant pattern in communication is the pathway along which messages are routed. Figure 5.5 illustrates a simple pathway.

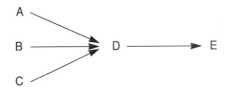

Figure 5.5   A communication pathway

A, B and C do not communicate directly with E: only D does that. D could be the mother of three children speaking with a worker, or a union representative talking to the boss. The pathway indicates the relative powerlessness of A, B and C to influence E, and the correspondingly relative powerfulness of D.

Patterns through time

Two questions about time are particularly helpful in determining the cause of social need:

> *When did it start?*
> *When does it occur now/When is it at its worst now?*

Many service users will themselves already have perceived the chronological context of the social needs that affect them. An older person may date their financial difficulties from the time they retired; a mother may recognise that her child is more truculent than usual on a Sunday evening, possibly following a weekend's access to their father or preceding a return to school.

Sometimes, however, service users are quite unaware of the chronological contexts which precipitate or perpetuate problems. It is then that a worker's experience or knowledge of social science theory can help to construct the missing association. A man may be vaguely aware that his anxiety states began a few years ago and now seem to 'come and go'. The worker might be able to pin the start down to a time when he feared that his wife was developing a relationship with another man. This causal relationship might be confirmed by the current association of his anxiety when his wife stays away from home overnight at conferences or other work commitments.

Causal relationships can also be inferred from the more detailed chronological sequences of everyday behaviour. One of the simplest sequences is the A – B – C:

- Antecedents
- Behaviour
- Consequences.

In this sequence, the problem behaviour, or event, is perceived in its temporal context as an attempt to replace the undesirable previous circumstances with the later, more desirable ones. Thus a child's temper tantrum may have been preceded by their mother and cohabitee starting to argue and been followed by a temporary adult cease-fire while they both attended to their child. Observing this sequence, workers and service users alike might recognise the causal link between the adult conflict and the tantrum.

Sequences are sometimes more involved and apparently circular in nature. A care assistant might observe that an older male resident often becomes abusive to the older women who share the same sitting area. This problem behaviour might be just one phase in a sequence such as that shown in Figure 5.6.

Many phases of this cycle could be experienced as problematic – for example, that the women feel the onus of having to include the man. However, only one of them has initially been identified as problematic by the worker. Having identified the cycle, the worker and service users will need, at the next phase, to plan where to seek to interrupt it.

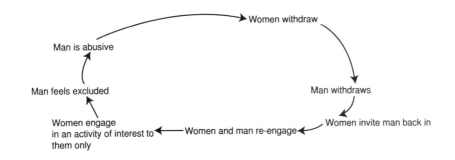

Figure 5.6   A behavioural sequence

Questions to ask in undertaking an assessment as a worker include:

Am I giving due weight to the service user's view of need?
Are there other workers whose views I should seek, within my agency or outside
it?
What are the main patterns *I can perceive which surround this social need?*

Planning

Planning plays a crucial role in the development of a structured, purposive sequence of events attempting to resolve social need (Fischer, 1978). All workers and service users have plans or 'purposes', even if embryonic and covert. However, if all the participants involved in resolving a social need are to play an appropriately full part, it is vital that plans are both developed and overt, through a shared process of open decisionmaking.

The NHS and Community Care Act (1990) has given the process of planning a new political meaning. Not only has it raised the level of public accountability, by requiring local authorities to publish their broader community care plans, it has also underscored the importance of 'care planning' as a phase which is separate from 'implementing the care plan' (DoH and Scottish Office, 1991b). The separation of both 'assessment' and 'planning' from 'implementation' is a central distinction in the increased privatisation of welfare.

Cordern and Preston-Shoot (1987a, pp. 20ff) argue strongly for the rights of service users to participate fully in the decisionmaking which is central to the planning process. However, the extent to which they seek to participate will vary according to expectations. Rees and Wallace (1982, pp. 39ff) suggest that some service users, often poor, expect to have less than an equal share in the decisionmaking process, while others, often well-educated and economically secure, expect to exercise more control over their own lives.

Service users' participation in the planning process will also be influenced by the extent to which the worker and/or their agency perceives the service user to be competent to participate. Children, for example, have too often been ignored in planning in the past (Reinach and Roberts, 1979; Page and Clark, 1977). It appears that they have been considered incompetent to contribute on the grounds of age and assumptions about limited understanding. However, more recent experiences of disclosure have taught professionals how reliable children can be, and organisations such as NAYPIC (National Association of Young People in Care) have fought to extend children's rights. Now the Home Office et al. (1991, p. 43) seek to encourage children to participate in case conferences whenever they have 'sufficient understanding and are able to express their wishes and feelings'. None the less, the Family Rights Group (1991) and others (Sone, 1991) still criticise the Children Act for not specifying an age at which children should be expected to attend such conferences.

Other service users can also be deemed incompetent to participate meaningfully in planning processes – for example, people with severe learning difficulties or suffering from dementia. However, independent advocacy schemes or training in self-advocacy can enhance their role. Sometimes, service users are excluded for more practical reasons: when the worker or agency does not seek to overcome any communication difficulty through sensory impairment, or when English is not a service user's first language. As Dominelli (1988) insists, getting a child to interpret for parents is not anti-racist practice.

The participation of parents at child protection case conferences is undoubtedly on the increase, although rather low levels have still been reported quite recently (DoH, 1991). Although Merchant and Luckham (1991) found that less opinion-giving and information-giving and more tension occurred when parents are present, Shemmings and Thoburn (1990) reported that participants did not usually feel inhibited themselves by the presence of parents, but thought that others might be.

Agencies and workers need to make considerable effort, often of a practical nature, in order to empower parents in child protection case conference planning (Driscoll and Evans, 1992). Parents could be prepared in advance, possibly in self-help groups, and allowed to bring a supportive advocate to the conference. Meetings can be arranged at times to suit all participants, not just regular core members, and at venues such as family centres or foster homes which are not intimidating or do not evoke unpleasant memories. Chairpersons can give parents sufficient time, ask appropriately clear, jargon-free questions and clarify the conduct of the meeting. Factors such as these could encourage service user participation in planning situations for all types of social need.

Service users' power can be further increased if plans are then recorded. Cordern and Preston-Shoot (1987a, pp. lxff) outline three main reasons for using written contracts:

1 enhancing the process of social work and enabling more effective outcomes, by clarifying goals and resolving clashes in perspective;
2 clients should be involved in deciding goals;
3 the process of reaching clear agreements can help workers to retain direction and all participants to explore conflicting views.

Their case has been forcefully attacked by Rojek and Collins (1987), who assert that there is an inherent balance of power against service users and in favour of workers by virtue of workers' knowledge, access to state resources and use of language, which contracts cannot redress. Cordern and Preston-Shoot's (1987b) reasonable response is that they do not expect contracts to change major structural disadvantage, but that they offer a small opportunity to redress power differences, through the processes of negotiating an agreed set of goals which can be made in the service user's language, sharing privileged knowledge and challenging the workers' discriminatory assumptions. Davies (1985) and Lishman (1994) also support the value of written contracts.

Nevertheless, the question remains as to how much the process of negotiation is genuine, when service users' choices are constrained by the threat of statutory action or by the absence of appropriate resources. Moreover, once the agreement is written, its binding power will only be evident in the redress service users can seek if it is not kept. Current community care (DoH and Scottish Office, 1991b, p. 67) and child protection guidelines (Home Office et al., 1991, pp. 32–44) both advocate written agreements. Time will tell how much they increase the power of service users.

Questions to ask are:

Am I certain that service users have participated in and agreed to these plans as much as they wish?
Have these plans been recorded and made accessible to service users?

Intervening

While all the preceding phases can lay effective foundations which satisfy service users as well as workers and agency managers, it is the intervention itself which offers them the primary opportunity to use their power appropriately to meet social needs. By 'intervention', we mean the action or actions taken specifically and directly to meet those needs, and not those other actions which prepare the way for that resolution. Intervention is the twice-weekly visits of the home care assistant to help an older person with problematic tasks, not the prior assessment visit of a community care manager or practitioner.

Service users speak clearly about the importance of this phase. Rees and Wallace (1982) report several studies in which service users speak of the acute disappointment they feel when, after some encouraging initial contact, the looked-for help with a social need does not materialise. Service users are also quite clear about the type of interventions they want. They appreciate an 'activist' approach in which the worker 'does things' for them – for example, giving advice, making practical arrangements, providing practical, material help. Even when subject to statutory interventions, service users indicate that they prefer openness, to be informed and to participate where possible.

We suggest that the fundamental principle for intervening in social care should be to maximise the service user's control whenever possible. This starts with a respect for the service user's choice from a range of options, even when it does not ultimately accord with the worker's or agency's. This is not to absolve paid workers and managers from their responsibility to suggest what they anticipate would be the most effective intervention, but to respect the service user's right to reject those suggestions.

Service user control also starts with strenuous attempts by workers and managers to adopt a voluntary intervention and resist a statutory one. This 'sub-principle' is clearly enshrined in both the Mental Health Act (1983) and the Children Act (1989). Even within a statutory intervention such as removing a child on an Emergency Protection Order, there will be innumerable smaller choices which parents and children can be encouraged to participate in – at what time, to what place, with what possessions, with what future contact, and so on.

Self-help can give service users considerable control. Adams (1990, p. 1) defines 'self-help' as both the individual and others 'coming together or sharing an experience or problem, with a view to individual and/or mutual benefit'. He further delineates three levels of the relationship between service users seeking self-help on the one hand and agencies and workers on the other (see Figure 5.7). The difference between levels is defined by the extent to which service users retain control over their helping process or cede it to workers and agencies. He argues that while integral self-help, with its higher level of control by agency and worker, might seem a contradiction in terms, all three levels can be effective in appropriate contexts.

Collective action is at the heart of self-help, just as it has been at the root of much political change. Sivandan (1991) and Dominelli (1988) describe the

Category of self-help	Resourcing by agency	Leadership by worker	Support by worker
Integral	Much or all	Direct	Regular
Facilitated	Some	Indirect	Intermittent
Autonomous	None	None	None

Source: Adapted from Adams, 1990, p. 34

Figure 5.7   Categories of self-help

solidarity and power which black people can derive from collective action. Other structurally powerless groups can assert their power through collective action. A fieldwork team in which one of the authors once worked combined with the other teams in that area to present a workload management scheme to agency managers which successfully reduced their workload pressures and ensured that prioritisation and accountability were forced up the hierarchy. It is unlikely that an individual worker or even an isolated team would have had the same impact.

It is noticeable that recent legislation has done little to encourage collective action on the part of service users. Holman (1992) suggests that a major flaw in the partnership between agency and service users advocated by the Children Act (1989) is that it is only encouraged at an individual level. While the NHS and Community Care Act (1990) does encourage the involvement of service user groups in strategic care planning, the evidence is that they have relatively little say in the face of the attitudes and power of statutory health and local authorities (King, 1991).

Agencies seek varying levels of control over the process of intervening. Managers will seek to control interventions, particularly when they are highly accountable for the use of expensive or scarce resources or for the risk to individual safety.

It is also the responsibility of managers to ensure that appropriate resources are available to meet the needs of their agency service users. This responsibility has been reinforced by the NHS and Community Care Act (1990) requirement that local authorities publish care plans which are developed through joint consultation. There are doubts about the effectiveness of this process, partly because of other events effecting local and health authority funding, such as the relationship between central and local government (Beardshaw, 1991), partly because of the variable relationships for partner-

ship due to past histories and the extent to which boundaries are cotermi-
nous, and partly because of the different methods of planning, sometimes as
a result of large-scale 'bottom-up' consultation involving service users and
workers at a local level (for example, in Islington, Humberside and
Wakefield), sometimes as paper exercises conducted by upper managers
(George, 1991).

There is a danger that the need for appropriate resources for black service
users will be lost in the jungle of joint planning for community care, particularly if, as is feared (George, 1991), smaller, innovative voluntary groups
which often spearhead such priorities have little or no voice in the planning.
Moreover, within the contract culture, small black groups are often disadvantaged in preparing a tender to provide resources (Sone, 1993).

Within such large-scale processes, it would be reasonable to assume that
individual workers have little control over interventions. It may be that in
some voluntary agencies, and even some local authorities, they are able to
influence the provision of resources through the development of community
care plans, as invited, or by collective action. They may also be in a position to
purchase appropriate resources if such decisions are delegated to care managers.

The interventions which workers can control most are those which stem
from themselves: an optimism about change which can match the service
users' initial hope for change (Rees and Wallace, 1982); their knowledge of
resources for that particular social need, both locally and wider; their interpersonal skills of counselling, advocacy, encouraging and persuading.

Workers are frequently called upon to exercise these interpersonal skills.
Although the majority of service users seem to expect practical help (Rees
and Wallace, 1982), there are many occasions when they voluntarily seek
help with interpersonal needs, or when agency managers and workers
encourage them to use such help in order to prevent the need for a statutory
intervention, or because they believe interpersonal needs underpin practical
ones. Many straightforward practical needs cannot be addressed without
initial interpersonal work – for example, persuading some older people that
it is their right and not a stigma to claim a given benefit. Consumer studies
(Rees and Wallace, 1982, pp. 61ff) suggest that service users from all socioeconomic groups seeking interpersonal help value not only the emotional
relief of talking with workers but also some positive action from the worker
in terms of advice, recommendation or prescription. This latter expectation
casts considerable doubt on ways of helping people with interpersonal needs
whereby workers offer no solutions and even prescribe 'apparent' problems
and not solutions, such as in Milan systemic therapy (Palazzoli et al., 1980).

The most effective action workers can frequently take is to encourage
service users to interact differently in the two modalities: behaviour and
thought. Feelings are not amenable to alteration at will, although they may

change as the other two modalities change. Service users can be asked to *behave* differently by undertaking new tasks together – for example, an older person's son may be encouraged to help perform some domestic duties hitherto undertaken solely by an overburdened daughter who despairingly sees no alternative to the older person going into a residential home.

The behaviour could also be one segment within a sequence of behaviours assessed as problematic. For example, a sequence in a residential home might be that an elderly resident appears withdrawn, a care assistant attempts to prod them into activity, the resident perceives it as nagging and withdraws further. The officer-in-charge might intervene by suggesting that the care assistant squats alongside the resident, then helps them out of their chair and onto another activity, rather than just standing over them and telling them to do something.

Another intervention to resolve this unhelpful sequence might equally have been for the officer-in-charge to encourage the resident to *think* of the care assistant's behaviour in a different way – 'She's not telling you off, she's just concerned that you seem so fed up with nothing to do.' The officer gives a more positive meaning to replace a more negative one (see Chapter 3). The worker's skill lies in perceiving this positive element even when service users only see the more negative side. Raynor and Vanstone (1994) describe a project which aims to alter the thinking of adult offenders.

The crucial difference between the two interventions above rests not so much in *how* the officer-in-charge intervenes, but *when* or *at what point* they intervene. In the first instance, they target the behaviour of the care assistant; in the second, the thoughts of the resident. An effective assessment will often guide the worker towards the most effective *point of intervention*.

More often than not, events can legitimately be construed in a number of ways, but people become fixed on just one unhelpful view. These views are often revealed in the details of their language. Modal verbs, for instance – such as 'must', 'should', 'ought to', 'can't', 'won't' – frequently reveal a fixed way of thinking which workers can sometimes encourage service users to change.

Questions to ask in intervening:

Has the service user sufficient control within this way of resolving their social need? If not, am I clear why not?

Are there ways in which this service user can usefully combine with other similar service users?

To what extent does the solution require a physical resource or the use of interpersonal skills?

Evaluating

Value is ascribed at every phase in the process of resolving social needs. However, the process of evaluating that we are particularly concerned with is that of placing a value on the *outcome* of the work process: did it work well or badly? While it is reasonable to suppose that well-executed processes at earlier phases are more likely to lead to a valued outcome, this result cannot be taken for granted. Assessments may be inaccurate, plans misguided, resources for effective intervention unavailable.

This differentiation between process and outcome is one which some service users find difficult to maintain (Rees and Wallace, 1982). When they do separate 'helpful people' from 'useful outcomes', they tend to attribute deficiencies in outcome to 'unhelpful' agencies which tend to limit the helpfulness of workers through excessive workloads and inadequate material resources.

A key question is:

> Who defines the value of an outcome?

As Sainsbury (1983, p. 2) suggests:

Welfare practices are potentially everybody's business.

There are many people quite distant from a given social need who may be concerned to judge whether an outcome is good or bad – agency upper managers, elected members, the media, the public, central government. It is interesting to observe how central government is increasingly controlling the definition of outcomes to be valued in education (e.g. through National Curriculum tests), while education workers, managers and children (as immediate service users and non-voters) have less say. It would seem that the government are taking an increasingly similar role with the personal social services, particularly as social services agencies fail to demonstrate that they are defining and monitoring outcomes to the government's satisfaction.

People more immediately involved in a particular social need who may be eager to define the value of an outcome include: the referred person, the referrer, immediate family or neighbours, the worker(s), line managers, other agencies' workers. A health visitor referred the 6-year-old son of a single, black mother, with her consent, to social services because of the boy's difficult behaviour and the mother's increasing frustration with it. The mother told the field social worker that her greatest worry was the racial harassment of her three children by a neighbour. The female, white worker found it more difficult to tackle the harassment than the boy's behaviour, and noted how unsupported the mother was. The worker's manager was predominantly satisfied that there was no substantial level of risk to the child. No one had discovered what, if anything, concerned the boy and the other two children. It is quite likely that all eight participants would have hoped for different outcomes.

How, in circumstances of such conflicting values, can workers ensure that service users have some power in defining a satisfactory outcome? First, the worker must seek to ensure that the service users' own presented needs have been met. Many workers and agency managers seek to evaluate the achievement of *goals* agreed by service users. These can be a helpful aid in evaluation, but goals are essentially constructed as a *means* to resolve the needs – the *ends*. Sometimes goals can be achieved, but needs still persist. For this reason, we suggest that, when evaluating, the worker should primarily focus on the resolution of needs.

A second way workers can ensure that service users' values are considered in appraising outcomes is to seek their statements of satisfaction, particularly in a way that minimises unhelpful bias (Evans et al., 1988). There is considerable debate in the consumer research literature (Rees and Wallace, 1982; Fisher, 1983; Cheetham et al., 1992) about the validity of service user satisfaction. Service users can have very low expectations and hence be easily and, according to commentators, inappropriately satisfied. Some commentators (Preston-Shoot and Williams, 1988; Sainsbury, 1983) prefer to concentrate on the effectiveness of outcomes – goals achieved, needs met – than service users' subjective statements of satisfaction. However, there is evidence that service users can still register satisfaction with processes which are ineffective in terms of goals achieved or needs met (Rees and Wallace, 1982).

We maintain that service users' statements of satisfaction are important, in addition to their evaluation of effectiveness. This is partly on the philosophical grounds that subjective statements of satisfaction are incontrovertible, unless the service user is lying, and that it would be inconsistent to value the service users' opinions in other respects but not in this one. It is also partly in recognition that social contexts are often highly complex, and the identification of needs and clarification of goals are both prone to miss other important variables. As the Barclay Report claims:

> It should be remembered that social work clients often have chronic problems and value social work not so much because they expect it to change their situation, but because they appreciate someone who recognises their difficulties and stands with them. (NISW, 1982, p. 173)

As well as the need to empower users within the process of evaluating, workers' own positions are in danger of being weakened by agency upper managers. Public accountability has led to an increase in agency systems of quality assurance. If workers are to achieve any autonomy in defining satisfactory outcomes, they will need to demonstrate to quality assurance units and their managers that their own systems of quality control are effective, through more rigorous processes of outcome evaluation.

More rigorous processes can be achieved not only by focusing on the criteria outlined above (effectiveness of needs resolution/goal achievement and service user satisfaction) but also by conducting outcome evaluation at a number of key points in time. In Figure 5.8, the three main criteria are mapped against five different points in time.

	Baseline	Continual	Review	End of contact	Follow-up
Identified needs	√	√	√	√	√
Agreed goals	√	√	√	√	√
Service user satisfaction		√	√	√	√

Figure 5.8   A model for outcome evaluation

Through assessing and planning, baseline problems are identified and goals agreed. Once an intervention begins, workers need to evaluate progress continually with service users: one simple question at the end of an interview, day attendance or week in residential care will often suffice. It is also helpful for workers or service users to initiate reviews of progress in longer-term interventions to prevent drift. There are requirements for formal reviews in statutory child care and child protection, although agency managers' values may predominate in such contexts. It is interesting that while community care guidelines support the value of reviews (DoH and Scottish Office, 1991b, pp. 83ff), they place more emphasis on small-scale reviews involving service users and workers, and less on large-scale, more formal agency reviews.

Many social needs reappear after contact with the worker and agency has stopped. For this reason, we consider that workers and agencies should attempt to follow up their work to demonstrate its continuing effectiveness.

This need not be an onerous task: a short phone call or supplying a reply-paid card may suffice. Both workers and managers have understandable fears about increasing workloads through follow-up contact. However, compensatory gains are, for the workers, a more accurate view of how effective their work is, and for the managers, evidence which allows them to consider the longer-term effectiveness of how they deploy resources. Service users who find their needs remain largely unmet will doubtless value such contact.

Questions to ask:

> *Is the service user having sufficient say in determining whether the outcome is satisfactory or not?*
> *What can I do to increase the service user's say?*
> *Do I need to encourage the service user to complain about the service they have received?*
> *Am I evaluating outcome frequently enough in this work?*

Ending

There seem to be two convincing reasons for focusing on this rather neglected final phase in the work process. There is evidence that service users are not always clear whether their contact with workers and their agencies has, in fact, ended or not (Cordern and Preston-Shoot, 1987a, pp. 14–15). Such uncertainty doubtless stems as much from workers' relative lack of attention to how work contact is ended as any other reason. Furthermore, it is during the process of ending that service users form their last and, sometimes, lasting impressions of social services agencies, which in turn can influence their expectations of and desire for future contacts. How many of us were taught to end our school or college essays with a punchy last paragraph to impress the marker?

As with all preceding phases, the key question is:

> *Who controls the ending?*

An impetus from a service user to end either voluntary or statutory contact before the agency has recognised the appropriateness of ending is prone to be interpreted as stemming from some other motive: 'resistance', 'avoidance', 'denial'. However, even when they are the unwilling recipients of statutory interventions, service users are clearly well placed to know whether an intervention has been effective so far, or whether the need for one has otherwise reduced. One important reform of the Children Act (1989, Section 29) was to impose a duty on local authorities to provide accommodation for children in need. This replaced the old category of 'voluntary care', which all too easily slid into an arrangement which parents or children could not easily end. As such, the new Act enshrines the service users' right to end a contact, unless a court has deemed otherwise.

Workers and managers may have their own agendas in seeking to end contact. The service users' circumstances may cause the worker personal or professional discomfort by resonating with similar social needs the worker has experienced, or they may make it difficult for the worker to feel effective and useful. Managers may wish to re-deploy their workforce in order to respond to some other perceived priority and thus be reluctant to allow worker and service user to complete the work to their mutual satisfaction.

A major aspect of work at this stage lies in ending a human relationship satisfactorily, since so much social care work and social work builds upon the formation of a relationship which service users clearly value (Rees and Wallace, 1982; Fisher, 1983). Workers may often concentrate on the loss which service users may experience – for example, by phasing out contact; exploring and validating feelings of loss; conducting an evaluation which realistically appraises the nature of the working relationship. Sometimes, too, it is important simply to allow service users to say goodbye in their preferred way, including a more informal farewell ritual.

It is not always easy to gauge which service users will appreciate a clear focus on ending. Some criteria are indicative: for instance, when the work has been concentrating on areas of loss through bereavement, disability, separation or change of accommodation; when the work has continued for some time or during major life upheavals; when the work has achieved major improvements. However, there will always be occasions when the worker cannot gauge this desire and must therefore give the service user satisfactory opportunity to end the contact. As part of the routine of leaving a job, one of the authors contacted all past service users with whom working relationships had not clearly ended. He was surprised to receive a lengthy letter from a black woman with whom he had worked some 18 months previously to resolve some difficulties her 4-year-old son was experiencing at a day nursery. The letter included many details about her life since that time, the progress that her son had made and thanks for the help received, and as such constituted her considered ending of the work contact.

Workers, too, have experienced losses in their lives and may have a similar need to end a particular working relationship well. Treacher (1989) describes graphically how his own experience of loss had clearly affected his work in ending therapeutic contact with his clients. Workers also have a strong need to clarify the extent of their achievement in their work before moving on to the next enterprise, particularly in a job where there are few obvious 'products' and which is constantly undermined by media and public disapproval and criticism.

Another relationship which requires some attention in this phase is the one between the referrer and the agency. Sometimes, the worker and/or service user will have been in regular contact with the referrer during the whole process, and they will thus be well-informed of the outcome. Often, this has not been the case, however, and it would seem good practice for the agency worker to notify the referrer of the outcome. In so doing, the worker respects the fact that referrers also have a concern for service users, and often much longer and more influential relationships with them. Moreover, this respectful last contact with the referrer over one piece of work may well influence the referrer's attitude towards making further contact with the agency. Such practice is standard in the medical world.

Questions to ask:

Am I allowing the service user to have sufficient say in when this work should end?

How much will I need to offer to concentrate on the emotional aspects of ending a human relationship?

How much are the agendas of my agency and myself in ending this work helpful or unhelpful?

Have I notified the referrer that this work has ended?

Every ending is a new beginning. In ending this book, we recognise that the ideas contained within it may develop in any number of directions. Any ideas you find helpful, you may develop in your work contexts or in relation to other interactional models.

It is uncertain how the context for systemic work will develop in the coming months or years. Recent legislation has placed considerable emphasis on increased partnerships between agencies and service users and between different sectors in the personal social services. Such emphasis, if resourced, could become a fertile soil for systemic approaches. However, the fourth consecutive term of Tory government seems to be continuing the emphasis on individualism, materialism and public expenditure cuts of its predecessors. If this predominant climate prevails, it will become crucial that less individualistic approaches are nurtured as an appropriate counterbalance.

References

Ackerman, N.W. (1958) *The Psychodynamics of Family Life*, New York, Basic Books.

Ackerman, N.W. (1966) *Treating the Troubled Family*, New York, Basic Books.

Adams, R. (1990) *Self-Help, Social Work and Empowerment*, London, Macmillan Education.

Ahmad, B. (1992) *Black Perspectives in Social Work*, Birmingham, BASW.

Ahmed, S., Cheetham, J. and Small, J. (1986) *Social Work with Black Children and their Families*, London, B.T. Batsford.

Andersen, T. (1987) 'The Reflecting Team: dialogue and meta-dialogue in clinical work', *Family Process*, 26, pp. 415–28.

Andersen, T. (ed.) (1990) *The Reflecting Team: Dialogues and Dialogues about Dialogues*, Broadstairs, Borgmann.

Arnstein, S.R. (1971) 'Eight Rungs on the Ladder of Citizen Participation' in Cahn, E.S. and Passett, B.A. (eds) *Citizen Participation in Effecting Community Change*, London, Praeger.

Ashby, W.R. (1952) *Design for a Brain*, New York, Wiley.

Atherton, J.S. (1986) *Professional Supervision in Group Care*, London, Tavistock.

Bailey, R. and Brake, M. (1975) *Radical Social Work*, London, Edward Arnold.

Bamford, T. (1989) 'Discretion and Managerialism' in Shardlow, S. (ed.) *Values of Change in Social Work*, London, Routledge.

Bamford, T. (1990) *The Future of Social Work*, London, Macmillan.

Barber, J. (1990) *Beyond Casework*, London, Macmillan.

Barber, S. (1991) 'Healing with Care', *Community Care*, 27 June (supplement), p. iv.

Barker, P. (1981) *Basic Family Therapy*, London, Granada.

Bateson, G. (1973) *Steps to an Ecology of Mind*, London, Paladin.

Bateson, G. (1979) *Mind and Nature*, London, Fontana/Collins.

Bateson, G., Jackson, D., Haley, J. and Weakland, J. (1956) 'Towards a Theory of Schizophrenia', *Behavioural Science*, Vol.1, No.4, pp. 251–64.

Beardshaw, V. (1991) 'Facing up to the Future', *Community Care*, 28 March (supplement), p. i.

Becker, H.S. (1963) *Outsiders: Studies in the Sociology of Deviance*, New York, The Free Press.

Bell, L., Bland, C. and Kearney, J. (1985) *Using the Systems Approach* (training video), Sunderland, Steam Training Co-operative.

Beresford, P. (1994) *Changing the Culture: Involving Service Users in Social Work Education*, London, CCETSW, Paper 32.3.

Beresford, P. and Croft, S. (1981) *Community Control of Social Services Departments*, London, Battersea Community Action.

Biehal, N. (1993) 'Participation, rights and community care', *British Journal of Social Work*, Vol.23, No.5, pp. 443–58.

Biestek, F. (1957) *The Casework Relationship*, Chicago, Loyola University Press.

Biggs, S. (1994) 'Up to All Angles', *Community Care*, 24 March, p. 24.

Blom-Cooper, L. (1985) *A Child in Trust: The report of the panel of inquiry into the circumstances surrounding the death of Jasmine Beckford*, London Borough of Brent.

Blom-Cooper, L. (1988) *A Child in Mind: The report of the commission of inquiry into the circumstances surrounding the death of Kimberley Carlile*, London Borough of Greenwich.

Boscolo, L., Cecchin, G., Hoffman, L. and Penn, P. (1987) *Milan Systemic Family Therapy*, New York, Basic Books.

Bradshaw, J. (1972) 'The Taxonomy of Social Need' in McLachlan, G. (ed.) *Problems and Progress in Medical Care*, Oxford, Oxford University Press.

Broderick, C. and Schrader, S. (1981) 'The History of Marital and Family Therapy' in Gurman, A. and Kniskern, D. (eds) *Handbook of Family Therapy*, New York, Brunner/Mazel.

Brook, E. and Davis, A. (eds) (1985) *Women, the Family and Social Work*, London, Tavistock.

Brown, A. (1984) *Consultation*, London, Heinemann.

Buckley, W. (1968) *Modern Systems Research for the Behavioural Scientist*, Chicago, Aldine.

Burke, A. (1986) 'Social Work and Intervention in West Indian Psychiatric Disorder' in Coombe, V. and Little, A. (eds) *Race and Social Work*, London, Tavistock.

Burnham, J. (1986) *Family Therapy*, London, Tavistock.

Butler, B. and Elliott, D. (1985) *Teaching and Learning for Practice*, Aldershot, Gower.

Butrym, Z. (1976) *The Nature of Social Work*, London, Macmillan.

Campbell, D. and Draper, R. (eds) (1985) *Applications of Systemic Family Therapy: The Milan Approach*, London, Grune and Stratton.

Carew, R. (1979) 'The Place of Knowledge in Social Work Activity', *British Journal of Social Work*, Vol.9, No.4, pp. 349–64.

Carpenter, J. (1984) 'Working Together: Supervision, Consultancy and Co-Working' in Treacher, A. and Carpenter, J. (eds) *Using Family Therapy*, Oxford, Basil Blackwell.

Carpenter, J. (1992) 'What's the Use of Family Therapy', *Australian and New Zealand Journal of Family Therapy*, Vol.13, No.1, pp. 25–32.

Carpenter, J. and Treacher, A. (1983) 'On the Neglected but Related Arts of Convening and Engaging Families and their Wider Systems', *Journal of Family Therapy*, Vol.5, No. 4, pp. 337–58.

Carpenter, J. and Treacher, A. (eds) (1989) *Problems and Solutions in Marital and Family Therapy*, Oxford, Basil Blackwell.

Carpenter, J. and Treacher, A. (eds) (1993) *Using Family Therapy in the 90s*, Oxford, Basil Blackwell.

Carr, A. (1986) 'Three Techniques for the Solo Family Therapist', *Journal of Family Therapy*, Vol.8, No.4, pp. 373–82.

CCETSW (Central Council for Education and Training in Social Work) (1989a) *Requirements and Regulations for the Diploma in Social Work*, London, CCETSW, Paper 30.

CCETSW (1989b) *Improving Standards in Practice Learning*, CCETSW, Paper 26.3.

CCETSW (1995) *Rules and Requirements for the Diploma in Social Work*, London, CCETSW (Paper 30, revised).

CCETSW/IAMWH (1989) *Multi-disciplinary Teamwork: Models of Good Practice*, London, CCETSW.

Chamberlain, E.R. (1977) 'Social Work: Practice Models and Theory Development', unpublished paper, Faculty of Social Work, University of Queensland.

Cheetham, J., Fuller, R., McIvor, E. and Petch, A. (1992) *Evaluating Social Work Effectiveness*, Buckingham, Open University Press.

Clarke, J. (ed.) (1993) *A Crisis in Care*, Milton Keynes, Open University Press.

Colwell Report (1974) *Report of the Committee of Inquiry into the Care and Supervision Provided in Relation to Maria Colwell*, London, HMSO.

Compton, B.R. and Galaway, B. (1979) *Social Work Processes*, Homewood, Illinois, The Dorsey Press.

Corby, B. (1992) 'Theory and Practice in Long-term Social Work', *British Journal of Social Work*, Vol.12, No.6.

Cordern, J. and Preston-Shoot, M. (1987a) *Contracts in Social Work*, London, Gower.

Cordern, J. and Preston-Shoot, M. (1987b) 'Contract or Con Trick? A reply to Rojek and Collins', *British Journal of Social Work*, Vol.17, No.6, pp. 535–43.

Cornwall, M. and Pearson, R. (1981) 'Co-therapy Teams and One-way Screen in Family Therapy Practice and Training', *Family Process*, Vol.20, pp. 199–209.

Coulshed, V. (1988) *Social Work Practice: An Introduction*, London, Macmillan.

Coulshed, V. (1990) *Management in Social Work*, Basingstoke, Macmillan.

Coulshed, V. (1991) *Social Work Practice: An Introduction*, 2nd edition, London, Macmillan.

Coulshed, V. and Adbullah-Zadeh, J. (1983) 'Case Examples of Family Therapy in a Social Services Department', *Social Work Today*, 17 May, pp. 11–15.

CRE (1977) *A Home from Home*, London, Commission for Racial Equality.

Croft, S. and Beresford, P. (1989) 'User Involvement, Citizenship and Social Policy', *Critical Social Policy*, Vol.2, pp. 5–18.

Dale, P., Davies, M., Morrison, T. and Waters, J. (1986) *Dangerous Families*, London, Tavistock.

Davies, M. (1977) *Support Systems in Social Work*, London, Routledge and Kegan Paul.

Davies, M. (1984) 'Training: What we think of it now', *Social Work Today*, 24 January, pp. 12–17.

Davies, M. (1985) *The Essential Social Worker*, 2nd edition, London, Wildwood House.

Davis, A. and Brook, E. (1985) 'Women and Social Work' in Brook, E. and Davis, A. (eds) *Women, the Family and Social Work*, London, Tavistock.

De Shazer, S. (1982) *Patterns of Brief Family Therapy*, New York, The Guilford Press.

De Shazer, S. (1985) *Keys to Solution in Brief Therapy*, New York, W.W. Norton.

Dell, P. (1982) 'Beyond Homeostatis; Towards a Concept of Coherence', *Family Process*, Vol.21, pp. 21–41.

DHSS (Department of Health and Social Security) (1978) *Social Services Teams: The Practitioners' View*, London, HMSO.

DHSS and Welsh Office (1988) *Working Together*, London, HMSO.

Dimmock, B. and Dungworth, D. (1983) 'Creating Manoeuvrability for Family/Systems Therapists in Social Work Departments', *Journal of Family Therapy*, Vol.5, No.1, pp. 53–69.

Dimmock, B. and Dungworth, D. (1985) 'Beyond the Family: Using network meetings with statutory child care cases', *Journal of Family Therapy*, Vol.7, pp. 45–68.

DoH (Department of Health) (1988) *Protecting Children: A Guide for Social Workers Undertaking a Comprehensive Assessment*, London, HMSO.

DoH (1991) *Patterns and Outcomes in Child Placement*, London, HMSO.

DoH (1994) *A Framework for Local Community Care Charters in England*, London, HMSO.

DoH and Scottish Office (1991a) *Care Management and Assessment: Summary of Practice Guidance*, London, HMSO.

DoH and Scottish Office (1991b) *Care Management and Assessment: Practitioners' Guide*, London, HMSO.

DoH and Scottish Office (1991c) *Care Management and Assessment: Managers' Guide*, London, HMSO.

Dominelli, L. (1988) *Anti-Racist Social Work*, London, Macmillan.

Dominelli, L. and McLeod, E. (1989) *Feminist Social Work*, London, Macmillan.

Dowling, E. (1979) 'Co-therapy: A clinical researcher's view' in Walrond-Skinner, S. (ed.) *Family and Mental Psychotherapy*, London, Routledge and Kegan Paul.

Doyle, M. and Straus, D. (1976) *How to Make Meetings Work*, New York, Jove Publications.

Driscoll, J. and Evans, L. (1992) 'An evaluation of the participation of parents and those with parental responsibilities in the child protection processes in Suffolk', Suffolk Area Child Protection Committee, unpublished.

Durkheim, E. (1938) *The Rules of Sociological Method*, New York, The Free Press.

Egan, G. (1982) *The Skilled Helper*, Monterey, California, Brooks/Cole Publishing Company.

Elliott, R. (1980) 'Conceptual Approaches to Power and Authority' in Lockett, M. and Spears, R. (eds) *Organisations as Systems*, Milton Keynes, Open University Press.

Ellis, K. (1993) 'Power Games', *Community Care*, 18 March, pp. 20–1.

Ely, P. and Denney, D. (1987) *Social Work in a Multi-racial Society*, Aldershot, Gower.

England, H. (1986) *Social Work as Art*, London, Allen and Unwin.

Erickson, G.D. (1988) 'Against the grain: decentring family therapy', *Journal of Marital and Family Therapy*, Vol.14, pp. 225–36.

Erickson, M.H. and Rossi, E. (1979) *Hypnotherapy: An Exploratory Casebook*, New York, Irvington.

Evans, D. (1985) 'Twosomes and Threesomes', *Community Care*, 24 January, pp. 16–18.

Evans, D. (1987a) 'Live Supervision in the Same Room', *Social Work Education*, Vol.6, No.3, pp. 13–17.

Evans, D. (1987b) 'The Centrality of Practice in Social Work Education', *Issues in Social Work Education*, Vol.7, pp. 83–101.

Evans, D. (1987c) 'Getting the Balance Right', *Community Care*, 11 June, pp. 18–19.

Evans, D. (1991) *Assessing Students' Competence to Practise*, London, CCETSW.

Evans, D., Cava, H., Gill, O. and Wallis, A. (1988) 'Helping Students Evaluate their own Practice', *Issues in Social Work Education*, Vol.8, No.2, pp. 113–36.

Evans, R.J. (1976) 'Some Implications of an Integrated Model of Social Work for Theory and Practice', *British Journal of Social Work*, Vol.6, No.2, pp. 177–200.

Family Rights Group (1991) *The Children Act 1989: An FRG Briefing Pack*, London, FRG.

Fennell, G., Phillipson, C. and Evers, H. (1988) *The Sociology of Old Age*, Milton Keynes, Open University Press.

Fernando, S. (1991) *Mental Health, Race and Culture*, London, Macmillan.

Fischer, J. (1978) *Effective Casework Practice*, New York, McGraw-Hill.

Fisher, M. (ed.) (1983) *Speaking of Clients*, Joint Unit for Social Services Research, Sheffield University.

Fisher, M. (1990) 'Case Management and Social Work: Clients with Dementia', *Practice*, Vol.4, No.4, pp. 229–41.

Francis, J. (1993a) 'Prejudice in Practice', *Community Care*, 11 March, pp. 14–15.

Francis, J. (1993b) 'A Colour-Conscious Approach', *Community Care*, 25 February, pp. 14–15.

Frederick, J. (1991) *Positive Thinking for Mental Health*, London, Black Mental Health Group.

Freud, S. (1973) *Introductory Lectures on Psychoanalysis*, London, Penguin.

Frost, N. and Stein, M. (1989) 'What's Happening in Social Services Departments?' in Langan, M. and Lee, P. (eds) *Radical Social Work Today*, London, Unwin Hyman.

Funnell, P., Gill, J. and Ling, J. (1992) 'Competence through Interprofessional Shared Learning' in Saunder, D. and Race, P. (eds) *Developing and Measuring Competence*, London, Kogan Page.

George, M. (1991) 'The Initiation Process', *Community Care*, 28 March (supplement), pp. ii–iii.

George, M. (1992) 'The Trouble about Complaining', *Community Care*, 9 April, pp. 16–18.

Gibson, P. and Robertson, K. (1988) 'Multi-disciplinary Assessment for Residential Accommodation', *Practice*, Vol.2, No.1, pp. 85–92.

Glaser, D., Furniss, T. and Bingley, L. (1984) 'Focal Family Therapy: The Assessment Stage', *Journal of Family Therapy*, Vol.6, No.3, pp. 265–74.

Goldberg, D. and Huxley, P. (1980) *Mental Illness in the Community: The Pathway to Psychiatric Care*, Columbia, South Carolina, University of South Carolina Press.

Goldner, V. (1985) 'Feminism and Family Therapy', *Family Process*, Vol.24, pp. 31–47.

Goldner, V. (1988) 'Gender and Generation: Normative and Covert Hierarchies', *Family Process*, Vol.27, pp. 17–31.

Goldstein, H. (1973) *Social Work Practice: A Unitary Approach*, Columbia, South Carolina, University of South Carolina Press.

Green, H. (1988) *Informal Carers: General Household Survey 1985*, London, HMSO.

Griffiths, R. (1988) *Community Care: An Agenda for Action*, London, HMSO.

Haley, J. (1971) 'A Review of the Family Therapy Field' in Haley, J. (ed.) *Changing Families*, New York, Grune and Stratton.

Haley, J. (1973) *Uncommon Therapy: The Psychiatric Techniques of Milton H. Erickson, M.D.*, New York, Norton.

Haley, J. (1976) *Problem Solving Therapy*, San Francisco, Jossey-Bass.

Hall, A.D. and Fagen, R.E. (1956) 'Definition of System' in Von Bertalanffy, L. and Rappaport, A. (eds) *General Systems Yearbook 1*, New York, Society of General Systems Research.

Hall, A.S. (1974) *The Point of Entry*, London, Allen and Unwin.

Handy, C.B. (1985) *Understanding Organisations*, 3rd edition, London, Penguin.

Hanmer, J. and Statham, D. (1988) *Women and Social Work: Towards a Women-centred Practice*, London, Macmillan.

Harding, T., Croft, S. and Beresford, P. (1993) 'The User Speaks', *Community Care*, 11 March, pp. 20–1.

Hare-Mustin, R. (1987) 'The Problem of Gender in Family Therapy Theory', *Family Process*, Vol.2, pp. 15–27.

Harrison, C. and Beresford, P. (1994) 'Using Users', *Community Care*, 24 March, pp. 26–7.

Hasenfeld, Y. (1992a) (ed.) *Human Services as Complex Organisations*, London, Sage.

Hasenfeld, Y. (1992b) 'Power in Social Work Practice' in Hasenfeld, Y. (ed.) *Human Services as Complex Organisations*, London, Sage.

Heron, J. (1975) *Six Category Intervention Analysis*, Human Potential Research Project, Guildford, University of Surrey.

Hodes, M. (1985) 'Family Therapy and the Problem of Cultural Relativism', *Journal of Family Therapy*, Vol.7, No.3, pp. 261–72.

Hoffman, L. (1981) *Foundations of Family Therapy*, New York, Basic Books.

Holman, B. (1992) 'Flaws in Partnership', *Community Care*, 20 February, pp. 15–16.

Holman, B. (1993) 'Too Poor to Care', *Community Care*, 11 February, p. 26.

Home Office, Department of Health, Department of Education and Science and Welsh Office (1991) *Working Together under the Children Act 1989*, London, HMSO.

Howe, D. (1987) *An Introduction to Social Work Theory*, Aldershot, Wildwood House.

Howe, D. (1989) *The Consumer's View of Family Therapy*, London, Gower.

Howe, D. (1992) 'Theories of Helping, Empowerment and Participation' in Thoburn, J. (ed.) *Participation in Practice – involving families in child protection*, Norwich, University of East Anglia.

Hugman, R. (1991) *Power in the Caring Professions*, London, Macmillan.

Ivory, M. (1994) 'Falling Short', *Community Care*, 31 March, pp. 21–2.

Jadeja, S. and Singh, J. (1993) 'Life in a Cold Climate', *Community Care*, 22 April, pp. 12–13.

James, K. and McIntyre, D. (1983) 'The Reproduction of Families: The Social Role of Family Therapy?', *Journal of Marital and Family Therapy*, Vol.9, pp. 119–29.

Johnson, D.P. (1981) *Sociological Theory: Classical Founders and Contemporary Perspectives*, New York, Wiley.

Johnson, T.J. (1972) *Professions and Power*, London, Macmillan.

Jones, C. (1983) *State Social Work and the Working Class*, London, Macmillan.

Jordan, B. (1975), 'Clients are fellow citizens', paper presented at BASW annual conference.

Jordan, B. (1979) *Helping in Social Work*, London, Routledge and Kegan Paul.

Jordan, B. (1981) 'Family Therapy: An Outsider's View', *Journal of Family Therapy*, Vol.3, pp. 169–80.

Jordan, B. (1987) *Rethinking Welfare*, Oxford, Basil Blackwell.

Kadushin, A. (1976) *Supervision in Social Work*, New York, Columbia University Press.

Kearney, J. (1986) 'A Time for Differentiation: The Use of a Systems Approach with Adolescents in Community-based Agencies', *Journal of Adolescence*, Vol.9, pp. 243–56.

King, J. (1991) 'Sharing the Power Game', *Community Care*, 11 July, pp. 15–18.

King, J. (1993) 'Walking a Tightrope', *Community Care*, 24 June, pp. 8–19.

Kingston, P. (1979) 'The Social Context of Family Therapy' in Walrond-Skinner, S. (ed.) *Family and Marital Psychotherapy*, London, Routledge and Kegan Paul.

Kingston, P. and Smith, D. (1983) 'Preparation for Live Supervision when Working without a One-way Screen', *Journal of Family Therapy*, Vol.5, pp. 219–33.

Kuhn, T.S. (1970) *The Structure of Scientific Revolutions*, Chicago, University of Chicago Press.

Laming, H. (1988) 'Corporate Identity', *Social Services Insight*, Vol.8, April.

Langan, M. (1985) 'The Unitary Approach: A Feminist Critique' in Brook, E. and Davis, A. (eds) *Women, the Family and Social Work*, London, Tavistock.

Langan, M. (1992) 'Women in the Mixed Economy of Care' in Langan, M. and Day, L. (eds) *Women, Oppression and Social Work*, London, Tavistock.

Langan, M. and Day, L. (eds) (1992) *Women, Oppression and Social Work*, London, Tavistock.

Langan, M. and Lee, P. (1989) *Radical Social Work Today*, London, Unwin Hyman.

Latham, T. (1982) 'The Use of Co-working (Co-therapy) as a Training Method', *Journal of Family Therapy*, Vol.4, No.3, pp. 257–70.

Lau, A. (1984) 'Transcultural Issues in Family Therapy', *Journal of Family Therapy*, Vol.6, No.2, pp. 91–112.

Leadbetter, D. (1993) 'Assaults on Social Work Staff', *British Journal of Social Work*, Vol.23, No.6, pp. 613–28.

Leonard, P. (1975) 'Towards a Paradigm for Radical Practice' in Bailey, R. and Brake, M. (eds) *Radical Social Work*, London, Edward Arnold.

Liddle, H. and Halpin, R. (1978) 'Family Therapy Training and Supervision: A Comparative Review', *Journal of Marriage and Family Counselling*, Vol.4, pp. 77–98.

Liddle, H., Breunlin, D. and Schwartz, M. (eds) (1988) *Handbook of Family Therapy Training and Supervision*, New York, The Guilford Press.

Lidz, T., Fleck, S. and Cornelison, A. (1965) *Schizophrenia and the Family*, New York, International Universities Press.

Lindsay, M. and Rayner, S. (1993) 'Balanced Judgements', *Community Care*, 1 July, pp. 24–5.

Lippitt, R., Watson, J. and Westley, B. (1958) *The Dynamics of Planned Change*, New York, Harcourt Brace.

Lipsett, D. (1980) *Gregory Bateson: The Legacy of a Scientist*, Englewood Cliffs, New Jersey, Prentice-Hall.

Lishman, J. (1994) *Communication in Social Work*, London, Macmillan.

Littlechild, B. (1993) 'Addressing Aggression', *Community Care*, 1 April, pp. 2–21.

Luepnitz, D.A. (1988) *The Family Interpreted: Feminist Theory in Clinical Practice*, New York, Basic Books.

MacGregor, R. (1962) 'Multiple Impact Psychotherapy with Families', *Family Process*, Vol.1, No.1, pp. 42–68.

MacGregor, R., Ritchie, A., Serrans, A., Schuster, F., McDonald, E. and Goolishian, H. (1964) *Multiple Impact Therapy with Families*, New York, McGraw-Hill.

MacKinnon, L.K. and Miller, D. (1987) 'The New Epistemology and the Milan Approach – Feminist and Sociopolitical Considerations', *Journal of Marital and Family Therapy*, Vol.13, No.2, pp. 139–55.

MacLeod, N.M. and Sagara, E. (1988) 'Challenging the Orthodoxy: Towards a Feminist Theory and Practice', *Feminist Review*, 28, January, pp. 16–55.

McNay, M. (1992) 'Social Work and Power Relations: Towards a Framework for Integrated Practice' in Langan, M. and Day, L. (eds) *Women, Oppression and Social Work*, London, Tavistock.

Madanes, C. (1981) *Strategic Family Therapy*, San Francisco, Jossey-Bass.

Madanes, C. (1984) *Behind the One-Way Mirror*, San Francisco, Jossey-Bass.

Mancoske, R. (1981) 'Sociological Perspectives on the Ecological Model', *Journal of Sociology and Social Welfare*, Vol.8, No.4, pp. 710–32.

Marchant, C. (1993) 'What Comes First?', *Community Care*, 15 July, pp. 18–19.

Maslow, A. (1970) *Motivation and Personality*, 2nd edition, New York, Harper and Row.

Mayer, J.E. and Timms, N. (1970) *The Client Speaks*, London, Routledge and Kegan Paul.

Merchant, A. and Luckham, S. (1991) *A Study of Parental and Child Participation in Child Protection Case Conferences in Mid Essex*, Chelmsford, Essex Social Services Department.

Miller, A.C. (1990) 'The Mother–Daughter Relationship and the Distortion of Reality in Child Sexual Abuse' in Perelberg, R.J. and Miller, A.C. (eds) *Gender and Power in Families*, London, Routledge.

Minuchin, S. (1974) *Families and Family Therapy*, London, Tavistock.

Minuchin, S. and Montalvo, B. (1971) 'Techniques for Working with Disorganised Low Socioeconomic Families', *American Journal of Orthopsychiatry*, Vol.3, pp. 880–7.

Minuchin, S., Montalvo, B., Guerney, B.G., Rosman, B.L. and Schumer, F. (1967) *Families of the Slums*, New York, Basic Books.

Mollica, R.F. and Mills, M. (1986) 'Social Class and Psychiatric Practice: A Revision of the Hollingshead and Redlich Model', *American Journal of Psychiatry*, Vol.143, No.1, pp. 12–17.

Montalvo, B. (1973) 'Aspects of Live Supervision', *Family Process*, Vol.12, pp. 343–59.

Morgan, G. (1986) *Images of Organisations*, London, Sage.

Morris, D. (1994) 'Time to Come in from the Cold', *Community Care*, 31 March, p. 18.

Morris, J. (1993) 'Criteria Motives', *Community Care*, 14 January, pp. 6–17.

Morris, K. (1994) 'Families in Conference', *Community Care*, 31 March, p. 27.

Morrison, C. (1988) 'Consumerism – Lessons from Community Work', *Public Administration*, 66, Summer, pp. 205–14.

Morrison, T. (1990) 'The Emotional Effects of Child Protection Work on the Worker', *Practice*, Vol.4, No.4, pp. 253–71.

Mouzelis, N. (1979) *Organisation and Bureaucracy*, 2nd edition, London, Routledge and Kegan Paul.

Mullen, E.G. and Dumpson, J.R. (1972) *Evaluation of Social Intervention*, San Francisco, Jossey-Bass.

Munday, B. (1989) *The Crisis in Welfare*, London, Harvester Wheatsheaf.

Neate, P. (1991) 'Putting it into Practice', *Community Care*, 28 March (supplement), pp. i–vii.

NISW (1982) *Social Workers: Their Role and Tasks*, London, Bedford Square Press.

O'Brien, C. (1990) 'Family Therapy with Black Families', *Journal of Family Therapy*, Vol.12, No.1, pp. 3–16.

O'Hanlon, W.H. (1987) *Taproots: Underlying Principles of Milton Erickson's Therapy and Hypnosis*, New York, W.W. Norton.

Olsen, M.R. (ed.) (1978) *The Unitary Model: Its Implications for Social Work Theory and Practice*, Birmingham, BASW.

Olsen, U. and Pegg, P. (1979) 'Direct Open Supervision: A Team Approach', *Family Process*, Vol.13, pp. 463–70.

Osborne, K. (1983) 'Women in Families: Feminist Therapy and Family Systems', *Journal of Family Therapy*, Vol.5, No.1.

Page, R. and Clark, G.A. (1977) *Who Cares?*, London, National Children's Bureau.

Palazzoli, M.S. (1984) Conference address to the Institute of Family Therapy, Cardiff, unpublished.

Palazzoli, M.S., Boscolo, L., Cecchin, G. and Prata, G. (1980) 'Hypothesising, Circularity and Neutrality: Three Guidelines for the Conductor of the Session', *Family Process*, Vol.19, pp. 3–12.

Paley, J. (1987) 'Social Work: The Sociology of Knowlege', *British Journal of Social Work*, pp. 169–86.

Parsloe, P. and Stevenson, O. (1993) 'A Powerhouse for Change', *Community Care*, 18 February , pp. 24–5.

Parsons, T. (1951) *The Social System*, Chicago, The Free Press.

Parton, N. (1985) *The Politics of Child Abuse*, London, Macmillan Education.

Payne, M. (1991) *Modern Social Work Theory*, London, Macmillan.

Payne, M. (1992) 'Routes to and through Clienthood and their Implication for Practice', *Practice*, Vol.6, No.3, pp. 169–80.

Perelberg, R.J. and Miller, A.C. (eds) (1990) *Gender and Power in Families*, London, Routledge.

Perlman, H.H. (1957) *Social Casework: A Problem-solving Process*, Chicago, University of Chicago Press.

Perrow, C. (1970) *Organisational Analysis: A Sociological View*, London, Tavistock.

Peters, G. (1993) 'On the Slippery Slope', *Community Care*, 25 May, pp. 14–15.

Phillimore, P. (1981) *Families Speaking*, London, Family Service Unit.

Phillips, D. (1983) 'Mayer and Timms Revisited: The Evolution of Client Studies' in Fisher, M. (ed.) *Speaking of Clients*, Joint Unit for Social Services Research, Sheffield University.

Philpott, T. (1994) 'Listen Who Cares', *Community Care*, 14 July, pp. 32–3.

Pilalis, J. (1986) 'The Integration of Theory and Practice: A Re-examination of Paradoxical Expectation', *British Journal of Social Work*, Vol.16, No.1, pp. 79–96.

Pilalis, J. and Anderton, J. (1986) 'Feminism and Family Therapy: A Possible Meeting Point', *Journal of Family Therapy*, Vol.8, No.2, pp. 99–114.

Pincus, A. and Minahan, A. (1973) *Social Work Practice: Model and Method*, Itarca, Illinois, F.E. Peacock.

Pithouse, A. (1987) *Social Work: The Social Organisation of an Invisible Trade*, Aldershot, Avebury.

Platt, D. (1993) 'The Age of Mutual Consent', *Community Care*, 22 April, pp. 20–1.

Preston-Shoot, M. and Agass, D. (1990) *Making Sense of Social Work: Psychodynamics, Systems and Practice,* Basingstoke, Macmillan.

Preston-Shoot, M. and Williams, J. (1988) 'Evaluating the Effectiveness of Practice', *Practice,* Vol.4, No.3, pp. 393–400.

Raymond, Y. (1989) 'Empowerment in Practice', *Practice,* Vol.1, No.1, pp. 5–23.

Raynor, P.G. and Vanstone, M. (1994) 'Probation Practice, Effectiveness and the Non-treatment Paradigm', *British Journal of Social Work,* Vol.24, No.3, pp. 387–404.

Rees, S. (1978) *Social Work Face to Face,* London, Edward Arnold.

Rees, S. and Wallace, A. (1982) *Verdicts on Social Work,* London, Arnold.

Reimers, S. and Treacher, A. (1995) *Introducing User-Friendly Family Therapy,* London, Routledge.

Reinach, E. and Roberts, G. (1979) *Consequences,* Portsmouth, Social Services and Intelligence Unit.

Richmond, M. (1917) *Social Diagnosis,* New York, The Free Press.

Rojek, C. and Collins, S. (1987) 'Contract or Con Trick?', *British Journal of Social Work,* Vol.1, No.2, pp. 199–211.

Rojek, C., Peacock, G. and Collins, S. (1988) *Social Work and Received Ideas,* London, Routledge.

Ross, S. and Bilson, A. (1989) *Social Work Management and Practice: Systems Principles,* London, Jessica Kingsley.

Rossi, E.L. (1980) (ed.) *The Collected Papers of Milton H. Erickson, M.D.* (4 volumes), New York, Irvington.

Rowlings, C. (1981) *Social Work with Elderly People,* London, Allen and Unwin.

Rubin, G. (1973) 'General Systems Theory: An organismic conception for teaching modalities of social work intervention', *Smiths College Studies in Social Work,* pp. 206–19.

Ruesch, J. and Bateson, G. (1968) *Communication: The Social Matrix of Psychiatry,* New York, W.W. Norton.

Sainsbury, E. (1970) *Social Diagnosis in Casework,* London, Routledge and Kegan Paul.

Sainsbury, E. (1983) 'Client Studies and Social Policy' in Fisher, M. (ed.) *Speaking of Clients,* Joint Unit for Social Services Research, Sheffield University.

Sainsbury, E., Nixon, S. and Phillips, D. (1982) *Social Work in Focus,* London, Routledge and Kegan Paul.

Seebohm Report (1968) *Report of the Committee on Local Authority and Allied Personal Social Services,* Cmnd 3703, London, HMSO.

Seed, P. (1973) *The Expansion of Social Work in Great Britain,* London, Routledge and Kegan Paul.

Shardlow, S. (ed.) (1989) *The Values of Change in Social Work,* London, Routledge.

Shemmings, D. and Thoburn, J. (1990) *Parental Participation in Child Protection Case Conferences: Report of a Pilot Project in Hackney SSD*, Norwich, Social Work Department Unit, University of East Anglia.

Sherman, W.R. and Wenocur, S. (1983) 'Empowering Public Welfare Workers through Mutual Support', *Social Work*, Vol.28, pp. 375–9.

Simons, K. (1993) 'A Chance to Speak', *Community Care*, 28 January, pp. 25–6.

Sivandan, A. (1991) 'Black Struggles against Racism' in Curriculum Development Steering Group (ed.) *Setting the Context for Change*, London, CCETSW.

Skynner, A.C.R. (1971) 'The Minimum Sufficient Network', *Social Work Today*, Vol.2, pp. 3–7.

Skynner, R. (1982) 'Frameworks for Viewing the Family as a System' in Bentovim, A., Barnes, G.G. and Cooklin, A. (eds) *Family Therapy: Complementary Framework of Theory and Practice*, London, Academic Press.

Smale, G., Tuson, G., Biehal, N. and Marsh, P. (1993) *Empowerment, Assessment, Care Management and the Skilled Worker*, London, HMSO.

Smith, N. (1991) 'Providing a Framework', *Community Care*, 27 June (supplement), pp. v–vi.

Sone, J. (1991) 'Crisis of Confidence', *Community Care*, 4 July, pp. 16–17.

Sone, K. (1993) 'Black Lives, White Perspectives', *Community Care*, 25 March, pp. 14–15.

Specht, H. and Vickery, A. (eds) (1977) *Integrating Social Work Methods*, London, Allen and Unwin.

Speck, R.V. and Attneave, C.L. (1971) 'Social Network Intervention' in Haley, J. (ed.) *Changing Families*, New York, Grune and Stratton.

Speck, R.V. and Attneave, C.L. (1973) *Family Networks*, New York, Pantheon Books.

Stanton, M.D. and Todd, T.C. (1981) 'Engaging Resistant Families in Treatment', *Family Process*, Vol.2, No.2, pp. 261–93.

Taggart, M. (1985) 'The Feminist Critique in Epistemological Perspective: Questions of Context in Family Therapy', *Journal of Marital and Family Therapy*, Vol.11, No.2, pp. 113–26.

Taylor, B. and Devine, T. (1993) *Assessing Needs and Planning Care in Social Work*, Aldershot, Arena.

Teismann, M.W. (1980) 'Convening Strategies in Family Therapy', *Family Process*, Vol.19, No.3, pp. 393–400.

Thomas, T. and Forbes, J. (1989) 'Choice, Consent and Social Work Practice', *Practice*, Vol.3, No.2, pp. 136–47.

Thompson, N. (1993) *Anti-Discriminatory Practice*, London, Macmillan.

Thoburn, J. (1980) *Captive Clients: Social Work with Families of Children Home on Trial*, London, Routledge and Kegan Paul.

Thoburn, J. (1992) 'Children's and Parents' Views on Participation' in

Thoburn, J. (ed.) *Participation in Practice – Involving Families in Child Protection*, Norwich, University of East Anglia.

Treacher, A. (1986) 'Invisible Patients, Invisible Families', *Journal of Family Therapy*, Vol.8, pp. 267–306.

Treacher, A. (1988) 'The Milan Method – A Preliminary Critique', *Journal of Family Therapy*, Vol.10, No.1, pp. 1–8.

Treacher, A. (1989) 'Termination in Family Therapy – Developing a Structural Approach', *Journal of Family Therapy*, Vol.11, No.1, pp. 135–47.

Treacher, A. and Carpenter, J. (eds) (1984) *Using Family Therapy*, Oxford, Basil Blackwell.

Triseliotis, J. (1987) 'Family Therapy or Working with Families', *Practice*, Vol.1, No.1, pp. 1–13.

Ussher, J.M. (1991) *Women's Madness: Misogyny or Mental Illness?*, London, Harvester Wheatsheaf.

Utting Report (1992) *Children in the Public Care: A Review of Residential Child Care*, London, HMSO.

Vickery, A. (1974) 'A System Approach to Social Work Intervention: Its Uses for Work with Individuals and Families', *British Journal of Social Work*, Vol.4, No.4, pp. 389–404.

Vickery, A. (1981) *Consultation on 64 Cases of Elderly People Living Alone Referred for Social Work Help*, London, NISW.

Virdee, G. (1992) 'Issues of Ethnicity and Participation' in Thoburn, J. (ed.) *Participation in Practice – Involving Families in Child Protection*, Norwich, University of East Anglia.

Von Bertalanffy, L. (1968) *General Systems Theory: Foundations, Development, Application*, New York, George Braziller.

Wallace, A. and Rees, S. (1984) 'The Priority of Client Evaluation' in Lishman, J. (ed.) *Evaluations*, London, Jessica Kingsley.

Walrond-Skinner, S. (1976) *Family Therapy: The Treatment of Natural Systems*, London, Routledge and Kegan Paul.

Walters, M. (1990) 'A Feminist Perspective in Family Therapy' in Perelberg, R.J. and Miller, A.C. (eds) *Gender and Power in Families*, London, Routledge.

Watzlawick, P., Beavin, J. and Jackson, D. (1967) *Pragmatics of Human Communication*, New York, W.W. Norton.

Watzlawick, P., Weakland, J. and Fisch, R. (1974) *Change: Principles of Problem Formation and Problem Resolution*, New York, W.W. Norton.

Weakland, J. (1974) ' "The Double-Bind Theory" by Self-reflexive Hindsight', *Family Process*, Vol.13, pp. 269–77.

Weissman, H., Epstein, I. and Savage, A. (1983) *Agency-based Social Work*, Philadelphia, Temple University Press.

Whan, M. (1983) 'Tricks of the Trade: Questionable Theory and Practice in Family Therapy', *British Journal of Social Work*, Vol.13, No.3, pp. 321–37.

Whitaker, C. (1967) 'The Growing Edge' in Haley, J. and Hoffman, L. (eds) *Techniques of Family Therapy*, New York, Basic Books.

White, M. and Epston, D. (1990) *Narrative Means to Therapeutic Ends*, New York, W.W. Norton.

Whiteley, P. (1994) 'Power to the People', *Community Care*, 7 September, p. 5.

Whittington, C. and Holland, R. (1985) 'A Framework for Theory in Social Work', *Issues in Social Work Education*, Vol.5, No.1, pp. 25–50.

Wood, W.H. (1989/90) 'A Systemic Approach to Protection', *Practice*, Vols 3 and 4, pp. 235–9.

Wynne, L. (1965) 'Some Indications and Contra-indications for Family Therapy' in Borzormenyi-Nagy, I. and Framo, J. (eds) *Intensive Family Therapy*, New York, Harper and Row.

Yelloly, M. (1980) *Social Work Theory and Psychoanalysis*, New York, Van Nostrand Reinhold.

Index